MANAGING STAFF
SELECTION AND ASSESSMENT

Paul Iles

Open University Press
Buckingham · Philadelphia

Open University Press
Celtic Court
22 Ballmoor
Buckingham
MK18 1XW

email: enquiries@openup.co.uk
world wide web: http://www.openup.co.uk
and
325 Chestnut Street
Philadelphia, PA 19106, USA

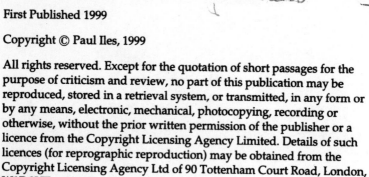

First Published 1999

A catalogue record of this book is available from the British Library

ISBN   0 335 19036 7 (pb)   0 335 19037 5 (hb)

Library of Congress Cataloging-in-Publication Data
Iles. Paul.
    Managing staff selection and assessment: prediction, interaction,
and control/Paul Iles.
    p.   cm. – (Managing work and organizations series)
    Includes bibliographical references and index.
    ISBN 0–335–19037–5 (hardcover). – ISBN 0–335–19036–7 (pbk.)
    1. Employee selection.   2. Employees – Rating of.   3. Executives –
Rating of.   4. Employment tests.   I. Title.   II. Series.
HF5549.5.S38144   1997
658.3'112 – dc21   97–30466   CIP

Typeset by Type Study, Scarborough

Printed and bound in Great Britain by
Marston Lindsay Ross International Ltd,
Oxfordshire

MANAGING STAFF
SELECTION AND ASSESSMENT

MANAGING WORK AND ORGANIZATIONS SERIES

Edited by Dr Graeme Salaman, Professor of Organisation Studies in the Faculty of Social Sciences and the Open Business School, the Open University

Current titles:

Peter Anthony: *Managing Culture*
Michael Armstrong: *Managing Reward Systems*
David Casey: *Managing Learning in Organizations*
Timothy Clark: *Managing Consultants*
Rohan Collier: *Combating Sexual Harassment in the Workplace*
Paul Iles: *Managing Staff Selection and Assessment*
Ian McLoughlin and Stephen Gourlay: *Enterprise Without Unions*
Graeme Salaman: *Managing*
Jenny Shaw and Diane Perrons: *Making Gender Work*
John Storey and Keith Sisson: *Managing Human Resources and Industrial Relations*

341504

CONTENTS

INTRODUCTION

The book begins by briefly discussing the components of the standard textbook model of selection and assessment – what we shall call the classical model of selection and assessment. It then discusses four different approaches to selection and assessment: the strategic management approach; the psychometric approach; the social process approach; and the critical discourse perspective on assessment. In discussing the strategic management approach we outline the way in which assessment and selection processes are linked to human resource planning and to organizational strategy, structure and culture. This link with strategy is then explored in some depth through a review of the reasons why leading organizations in the private and public sectors have realized the crucial strategic role of selection and assessment processes and revamped their assessment strategies and practices in the light of environmental changes. In this way, it is argued, assessment and selection processes can not only aid immediate selection decisions but can also assist in the selection of development activities, enhance human resource planning and career management, and help in the appraisal of potential. The book presents a framework linking assessment processes to corporate strategy, as in many cases environmental changes will lead to a redefinition and reorientation of strategy and changes to

1

organizational structure and organizational culture, with consequent impacts on the design of jobs and roles and the knowledge, skills and other requirements for such jobs. Job analysis, especially if of a strategic, future-oriented kind, may help identify what these requirements may be, leading to the design of appropriate person specifications and the choice of appropriate selection and assessment methods. This it is claimed, can enable the most appropriate match to take place between individuals and organizations, as well as enabling the identification of training and development needs.

The book then uses this framework to explore in more depth a number of issues: whether to match managers to strategy and how best to achieve this; how to take the assessment implications of job redesign into account; how best to assess future trends and their implications for job roles; and how to take equal opportunity and diversity considerations into account at all stages of the assessment and selection process.

Having set the strategic framework for selection and assessment, the psychometric model is then introduced through an examination of a number of assessment methods and procedures available to organizations. The standards or criteria by which these methods and procedures could be judged are reviewed. Noting differences in assessment and selection practice between different countries, the book points out that the most frequently used techniques are not necessarily regarded as the most valid, reliable or bias-free, and goes on to compare selection methods in terms of other criteria such as utility, acceptability and impact. The book then reviews the social process model of assessment and explores a critical discourse perspective on the relationship between assessment processes, knowledge, and power. It concludes by applying such frameworks to an area of current importance: the identification, assessment and development of managerial competence.

Assessment processes are widely used in organizations to recruit, select, place, promote and develop individuals and to support and facilitate organizational, cultural and strategic change. In this book we will limit our discussion of assessment to individual psychological assessment, rather than also focus on organizational assessments of various kinds (e.g. attitude surveys, quality assessments and culture audits). This kind of assessment is clearly also important to the enhancement of organizational effectiveness. We will, however, not restrict ourselves to traditional assessment concerns with recruitment, selection and promotion but will also review the role of individual assessment in promoting and supporting organization-wide programmes of strategic and cultural change, as well as facilitating individual change and development.

Staff selection and assessment

In this book assessment is seen as involving the relatively systematic, standardized collection and evaluation of information from individuals regarding their characteristics, skills, knowledge, competencies and other attributes in order to make job, career and other organizational decisions. Such decisions include recruiting a person, selecting a person for a job, placing an individual in a role, project or team, transferring a person to another role, promoting an individual, redeploying or deselecting an individual, identifying individual training and development needs, and profiling and auditing human resources as a precursor to organization development initiatives, such as programmes of cultural change, strategic realignment, restructuring, or total quality management.

In the classical model of assessment, the *outcomes* of assessment processes typically include a comparison of an individual's characteristics, attributes, behaviour, knowledge, competencies and styles with a set of *criteria* or standards in order to make *predictions* about that individual. These predictions may include predictions of job performance, job fit, team compatibility, development potential; of relevant development opportunities to help bridge knowledge or skill gaps; or predictions of organizational 'readiness' for large-scale change efforts.

In general, the kinds of typical assessment processes we will focus on involve the prediction of work-related job, career and organizational behaviour, and utilize such dimensions or constructs as behaviour, skills, personality characteristics and traits, behavioural styles, cognitive abilities, interests and motivations.

3

A major focus in recent years has been on the concept of occupational, especially managerial *competence*, discussed extensively in Chapter 5. The assessment tools, techniques and procedures that we will review in Chapter 3 include interviews (in particular, structured and unstructured interviews), psychological tests (in particular, tests of cognitive ability), psychological inventories (in particular, work-related questionnaires, questionnaires of managerial, leadership, thinking and learning styles, and assessments of team roles and preferences) and behavioural simulations (such as work samples and assessment centres). Such techniques show different patterns of use across regions and countries, and exhibit different degrees of bias or adverse impact against different social groups – issues that will also be discussed in Chapter 4.

The distinctiveness of the book

The book is distinctive in several ways:

- It introduces an explicitly *strategic* dimension to the discussion of staff selection and assessment, and locates this area clearly within current conceptions of human resource management (HRM).
- It introduces an explicitly international focus to its discussion of staff selection and assessment practices.
- It explicitly incorporates a discussion of equal opportunity and diversity issues in assessment practice, rather than seeing them as marginal and peripheral to the discussion.
- It explicitly reviews and compares the assumptions underlying four major approaches to selection and assessment practice – the psychometric model rooted in differential psychology, the social process model rooted in social psychology, the critical discourse model rooted in sociology and critical theory, and the strategic model rooted in strategic management theory. It then applies these frameworks to an important area of current concern, the identification, assessment and development of managerial competence.

- It focuses on the management of assessment, not on the technical competence of carrying out assessments in practice, or the technical issues of measurement and validation.

1

DIFFERENT PERSPECTIVES ON ASSESSMENT AND SELECTION

The classical approach

The conventional model of assessment, derived primarily from psychometric psychology, argues that organizations need to determine the numbers and kinds of people to be recruited at specific times, while job positions need to be defined in terms of the skills, competencies and abilities required to perform critical job functions. People with the relevant knowledge, skills and abilities for these positions will then need to be identified, attracted and placed appropriately. All of these activities involve the *assessment* of people and the matching of people with jobs. The standard approach to assessment in organizations therefore involves several components.

Human resource planning

Human resource planning (HRP) is the process by which the organization's human resource requirements are reviewed in order to achieve organizational goals through having the requisite number of individuals with appropriate skills available when needed. Forecasting human resource requirements is intended to enable the number, skills and positions of necessary employees to be determined. Forecasting availability is intended to enable potential sources of supply, both internal and external, to be identified. It is often argued that this process must be successfully carried out before other assessment activities can be undertaken, though in practice this is rarely done.

Job analysis

Job analysis refers to the process whereby information about jobs, roles and positions within the organization is systematically gathered and the skills, abilities and knowledge required for successful performance identified. Job analysis is usually regarded as an essential first step for many other HRM functions, such as performance appraisal, training and development and job design and redesign. It is regarded as necessary to prepare job descriptions and person specifications on which to base recruitment and selection strategies, as well as to develop the criteria by which the effectiveness of the recruitment and selection procedure can be judged. It is increasingly argued that a *strategic* approach to job analysis is necessary, as we shall see in Chapter 2. Again, in practice systematic job analysis is rarely carried out before recruiting and selecting employees.

Recruitment

Recruitment involves the attraction of people, both inside and outside the organization, in sufficient numbers and with relevant skills and knowledge, to apply for appropriate jobs. Recruitment may be carried out by a variety of methods, including the use of advertising, employment agencies, and search and selection firms.

Selection and placement

The selection and placement process may be carried out in different ways, such as scrutinizing application forms and curriculum vitae (résumés), carrying out preliminary and further interviews, testing for ability and personality, using assessment centres, and obtaining and checking references. Selection and assessment techniques will be reviewed later in the book in relation to the standards available to judge their effectiveness. These include the predictive validity of the techniques, or their ability to make accurate predictions of successful job performance; their utility or cost effectiveness; and their degree of bias or adverse impact against particular groups. The relevance of equal opportunity considerations – legislation, codes of practices, and guidelines – for the recruitment and selection process will also be discussed. Again, in practice such considerations may only rarely be taken into account.

Career and performance management

The assessment process is also concerned with employees after they have become organizational members, and with ensuring that they have the opportunities available to maximize their potential. High levels of productivity and organizational effectiveness can only be achieved, it is argued, when jobs, career paths and individuals are properly aligned – if such a process is at all feasible.

Assessment activities alone, of course, will not ensure organizational effectiveness. They will need to be integrated with programmes of training and development, job and work design, organizational climate and cultural change, leadership style and communication and motivation, including reward and compensation activities. In practice, very few of the components outlined above are considered when making recruitment, selection and promotion decisions. Recruitment is often expedient, not informed by HR forecasts or job analyses. Some of the reasons for this and some of the complexities involved in managing assessment will be explored later in the book.

Organization development and human resource development

The classical model has typically focused on *individual* assessment for recruitment and selection purposes, while strategic

8

management focuses more on *organizational* development and organizational change. Assessment is increasingly claimed to be a key vehicle for diagnosing needs for organization development efforts and human resource development activities. Audits of the knowledge, skills and abilities of sections, departments or the entire organization may lead to the need to revise strategic direction, recruit more external staff, or engage in more systematic development efforts. Assessing teams can lead to more informed team building and team development efforts. For example, the Myers–Briggs Type Indicator is often used to reveal issues of team communication or team balance, while questionnaires such as personality inventories or the Belbin team role inventory (Belbin 1981) are often used to reveal the characteristic roles and styles adopted by people in teams. This is claimed to help in team selection, in selecting individuals for project teams, and in identifying team training needs and strategies for team development.

Assessment has also been considered to play a key role in situations like mergers and acquisitions, where the human resources of two organizations are to be merged. Assessing the target organization prior to merger or acquisition may reveal skill strengths or identify potential 'culture clashes', whereas assessing the acquiring organization prior to merger may help reveal deficiencies and areas where merger and acquisition may help strengthen skills and capabilities.

Organizational change

Assessment may also play a role in facilitating organizational change. Carrying out a strategic job analysis to identify 'the success factors' required in the future allows existing staff skills to be profiled and audited. This in turn allows development initiatives to be targeted towards building future capabilities and permits staff to be assessed in terms of their ability to succeed in the 'new' organization. It is even possible to devise simulations such as assessment centre activities to provide a taste or 'virtual reality' experience of what that organization might look and feel like, and what qualities are needed to be successful in it.

This discussion of organizational change shows the importance of considering the strategic direction of the organization, since assessment criteria and practices will need to change as organizational strategies change and new skills and competencies are emphasized. We will therefore need to consider the strategic context of assessment and the relationship between assessment processes and various aspects of corporate strategy. We therefore need to take a more *strategic* perspective towards the management of assessment procedures, and in particular to explore their links with corporate strategy. This is an area considered in more depth in Chapter 2.

Purposes and benefits of assessment: the claims of the classical model

Organizations have engaged in assessment activities for a variety of reasons and to achieve a variety of purposes, and have cited a number of benefits from doing so. The main benefit claimed for the classical model of assessment is that it provides for standardized, objective evaluation of people in contrast to the subjective, perhaps biased assessments made by organizational decision makers relying solely on track record, hearsay, personal experience and subjective judgement. For example, it may be claimed that assessment reduces class, gender or racial bias in selection decisions. It may also be claimed that assessment promotes more meritocratic selection, ensuring that only job-relevant skills and qualities are taken into account in reaching selection decisions. Using a variety of assessment techniques can provide multiple perspectives on a person's skills, knowledge and other relevant qualities. In this way, it is claimed, psychological assessment can improve the effectiveness of a variety of human resource decisions and reduce the cost of errors in such decisions.

A systematic, thorough job analysis may enable the job description to accurately describe job duties and results, and may enable a person specification to be drawn up containing a full, comprehensive description of the skills, knowledge, competencies and other characteristics being sought. Appropriate assessment methods may then be used to identify whether candidates do in fact display such qualities, and more effective placement and promotion decisions may then be taken. If a strategic job analysis is carried out, criteria deemed relevant in the future as well as in the present can be included. For example, it is not always helpful to use past behaviour, as judged by track record or appraisals to make predictions about behaviour in a new situation, such as where a new job is significantly different from the last. Such discontinuities in career paths may make the kinds of characteristics and qualities necessary for success in the new job quite different from those required for success in the old job. Promoting the best performer in the old job to the new position (e.g. best production employee to supervisor, best R & D scientist to R & D manager, best engineer to manager, best supervisor to manager of managers) may mean that the organization both loses a good engineer, scientist, supervisor or production worker and that it gains a poor manager. Similarly, moving from managing a business function to a general management role, moving from managing one type of business to multiple types of business, moving laterally to a job with a quite different content, or moving from a domestic managerial role to an international one all involve significant discontinuities. Here past performance alone may again not predict future success in a changing work environment. Assessment of the characteristics required by the new job and of the degree to which the person can exhibit them may help make such transition decisions more effective.

It is not only jobs that change; people do too – a contention of particular importance to the social process model discussed later in the book. Their competence can be developed and their skills enhanced through maturity, experience, job changes, and focused training and development initiatives. Reassessing people periodically may help organizations understand and capture such changes and help them re-focus their training and development initiatives.

Organizations are also changing, displaying considerable re-engineering and restructuring, at least in rhetoric if not always in reality. Structures are being redesigned, cultures transformed, leadership models reconsidered, and team relationships re-thought. Assessment processes may help to assess the readiness and suitability of people for these new roles and help identify people who have the skills and competencies to meet changing demands and cope with constant change. Assessment processes may also help people to picture and understand the desired changes required by the organization more clearly and to appreciate the new skills and behaviours required for success more fully, allowing them to make decisions as to whether to continue with the changing organization or to seek a role outside it.

In this respect assessment processes are also claimed to help facilitate individual development and change, since they can provide a powerful source of feedback about behaviour to individuals. This feedback may be otherwise hard to come by in organizations. Assessment provides, in addition to feedback from performance appraisal and review, a context in which to situate and understand skills and competencies. Such self-knowledge may be a pre-requisite for targeted and focused development efforts. Whether self-driven or organization driven, assessment data may provide an informed base for both organization and human resource development initiatives.

Finally, it is claimed that assessment processes can help enhance organizational effectiveness by improving the quality of employees and improving the fit between people and organizations, thereby improving quality and productivity and reducing turnover. In the rest of the book we will evaluate critically the evidence for such claims through an analysis of four different perspectives on assessment and selection. Since this book is concerned with the *management* of staff selection and assessment, we will begin with a discussion of organizational strategy and change and its links with assessment (what we will term the strategic model of assessment) after a brief introduction to the four models considered in this book.

Four perspectives on the assessment process

This book presents an approach to selection and assessment processes which draws on four disciplinary perspectives (American differential psychology, European social psychology and postmodern critical sociology, and American strategic management theory) and which links two functional disciplines (human resource management and strategic management).

First, we explore the approach to assessment stemming from

strategic management, noting how companies have begun to place assessment and selection higher on their corporate agenda and have sought to link assessment processes both internally or horizontally with other HRM policy areas like training or reward and externally or vertically with corporate strategy. Most discussion in this area has been dominated by a rather reactive, 'matching' model of strategic assessment: the notion that organizations need to 'match' their assessment strategy (what criteria to look for, what methods to employ, etc.) to their generic corporate strategy (e.g. cost leadership, differentiation and focus) and also to their structure and/or to their life-cycle stage and/or their corporate culture. More recently, the resource-based view of strategic management, which places less emphasis on industry structure and competitive environment and more emphasis on internal resources and capabilities as the cornerstone of strategic management, promises to offer assessment a more proactive role, in that the skills, knowledge and attributes of employees are seen as central to sustainable competitive advantage, requiring that close attention be given to their assessment. In addition, innovative, distinctive and hard to imitate HRM practices, such as assessment and selection practices, may also constitute a set of organizational capabilities that can lay the basis for sustainable competitive advantage.

Secondly, we review the strengths and weaknesses of the dominant American psychometric paradigm of selection and assessment, focusing on job analysis, performance criteria, individual attributes and the prediction of job performance. We then discuss the appropriateness of this model and discuss the challenges posed to it by an emerging European social process model rooted in social psychology and interactionist sociology and focusing on interaction, negotiation, influence, identity and relationships.

Thirdly, we then evaluate both models in the light of perspectives drawn from conceptions of post-modernism and the role of assessment technologies in regulation and control, as aspects of a discourse of organizational government (drawn from critical theory and sociology).

Our concern is to describe, contrast and evaluate these approaches; the focus is on how the activity of managing selection and assessment is seen and constructed in four very different models, each of which draws on very different and, in some cases, opposing epistemological and methodological perspectives. These approaches we shall term 'paradigms', partly in the sense that they represent often opposing, perhaps incommensurable world views, but also because they represent perspectives which inform both practitioners and researchers as to what questions to ask about assessment, what methods and techniques to use in addressing them and what criteria to use in assessing what counts for valid knowledge about assessment.

These approaches differ widely; they are not just different ways of seeing the same thing, but differ epistemologically. Two in particular fundamentally question the basis on which the others make knowledge and truth claims. Psychometric psychology claims to be able to identify and measure the critical human dimensions that affect work performance. The only problems it acknowledges are technical issues of the definition of traits, dimensions and competencies, and the quality of the tools of measurement. The discourse approach, on the other hand, regards the 'psychometric' approach and all its associated techniques, dimensions, instruments, methods, and practices as a discourse – a way of knowing, measuring and constructing individuals and their key, relevant qualities. This approach regards the qualities, dimensions, attributes, isolated and measured by psychometrics as *constructed* by psychology and psychometrics, both of which are seen as providing just one, albeit often privileged form of language. The authority of science – in this case, psychology and psychometrics – is seen as depending not on its claims to the identification of essential inherent truths, but on the way in which it presents itself. The achievement of scientific authority not only implies a claim to be heard; it also implies a successful attempt to define how claims should be presented and judged. This approach sees itself as entirely undermining the 'authority' and truth claims of psychometrics. The concerns of the psychometric approach – and of many who have criticized it in terms of the efficiency of the approach, the validity of its instruments, the bias of its assumptions, etc. – are in themselves of interest from a discourse point of view only to the extent that these criticisms support the very assumptions on which the approach is based. These criticisms critique the success of the approach, but not its possibility; nor do they question the nature and basis of the knowledge on which the approach is based.

The social process approach sits somewhere in the middle. On the one hand, it argues that the psychometric-objective approach is unrealistic, if not unreasonable, insisting that in practice those involved in selection processes use available technologies, dimensions and criteria not to determine and structure activity and decisions but to make sense of such activity. On the other hand, this approach falls considerably short of the insistence of the discourse approach that the psychometric approach is a form and technique of government, seeing it as a case of 'the diversity of powers and knowledge entailed in rendering a field practicable and amenable to intervention' (Miller and Rose, 1993: 77). It could, however, be argued that in its own way the social process approach does adhere to a major tenet of discourse analysis: that the psychology of selection and assessment is 'a body of knowledge that has been *produced* rather than *discovered*' (Holloway, 1991: 1, our emphasis).

These points are developed later in the book, and applied to the analysis of managerial competencies in particular as an illustration of the strengths and limitations of each approach. We first discuss the four models in more detail.

The strategic management perspective

Most approaches to the strategic management of assessment, as we have seen, lay stress on the need to 'match' assessment strategy to generic corporate strategy, life cycle, structure or culture. Such a conception, popular in the late 1980s and early 1990s, places assessment in a rather secondary, downstream and reactive role, though such models remain popular among both line and personnel managers.

However, alternative perspectives on assessment can be taken from the strategic management literature, in particular the emerging 'resource-based view of the firm'. In this view, the emphasis is less on industry structure and competitive environments (an emphasis in 1970s and 1980s strategic management theory) and more on the internal resources of the firm as a source of sustainable competitive advantage. The focus here is on tangible and intangible resources (including of course human resources), and in particular employee skill-pods, core competencies and organizational learning. Firm resources might be classified as tangible (e.g. physical, financial), intangible (e.g. reputation, brand, image) organizational (e.g. processes and systems) or human (e.g. knowledge, skills competencies). Organizations are seen as comprising very different collections of assets and capabilities, which in turn affect performance. Successful companies are seen as having the most appropriate stocks of resources for their selected strategy. Sustainable competitive advantage is therefore seen as ultimately attributable to ownership of competitively distinct, well-deployed and valuable resources (e.g. Grant, 1991; Wright *et al.*, 1994; Hamel and Prahalad, 1994).

However, such a view is not solely inward-looking, an over-compensating correction to the external focus of earlier strategic management theory. To be a source of sustainable competitive advantage, such resources need to be appraised in the light of the external competitive environment, and they need to be integrated, coordinated and deployed as *distinctive capabilities* or *core competencies*. Resources are seen as being subject to the market forces of demand, scarcity and appropriability. They must be scarce, relevant, durable, inimitable, non-substitutable, and competitively superior; durability and inimitability in particular are seen as central to *sustainable* competitive advantage. There also needs to be continual investment and upgrading of resources, and leveraging of resources into effective strategies in new industries and new markets. Firms often appear to over-estimate both their ability to compete in attractive industries and their ability to leverage generic resources as a source of competitive advantage in new markets. A key issue is also *appropriability*; who captures the value from the resource? Is it the firm, or is it its employees, customers and suppliers, or is it the government, for example?

This approach argues that in a dynamic and uncertain external environment, identifying, developing and exploiting internal resources and capabilities may be a more secure foundation for strategic direction; specific markets or products are seen as secondary considerations (e.g. Canon's focus on imaging, microelectronics, fibre optics and precision engineering rather than cameras or copiers). The success of Japanese companies is often attributed not to their product management skills, but to their competence or capability management skills. Resources are not seen as productive on their own, but need to be put together in the form of capabilities or competencies in order to undertake activities. The key strategic issue is seen as competition around distinctive, superior capabilities, relative to other firms; this perspective is therefore often known as the 'resource-capability' perspective. This book will go on to apply resource-capability perspectives on sustainable competitive advantage to assessment issues, especially to issues of managerial competence.

The psychometric perspective

Research and practice in the field of selection and assessment has long been dominated by one particular paradigm in occupational psychology (Hollway, 1991). This is the 'psychometric' approach which has its roots in 'differential psychology', the study of consistent patterns of individual differences, developed in particular in the United Kingdom in the late nineteenth century. This approach to individual psychology is rooted in a positivist, empiricist tradition which seeks to discover objective 'facts' about people by the application of rigorous scientific methods. In the United Kingdom this approach has been less linked to the environmentalist, experimental tradition dominant in the United States of America, especially in the 'behaviourist' tradition of Watson and Skinner, and much more closely aligned to a nativist, genetic perspective on the origins of individual differences and to the development of sophisticated statistical techniques to analyse 'mental differences'. Perhaps echoing the British class system, belief in the imperialist mission and a subscription to a belief in 'innate differences', its primary focus has been on differences in 'general intelligence'. Though its initial application was to education (where the original diagnostic 'developmental' emphasis of Binet was transformed into an emphasis on selection and streaming under the influence of Burt and others), it became particularly influential in selection practice after World War I when intelligence tests were used to place people rapidly into jobs.

The tradition has broadened and embraced other concerns in the twentieth century. In the United States of America it has shown interest in more specialized mental abilities rather than in general mental ability alone, as well as an interest in other cognitive dimensions such as creativity, cognitive styles and learning styles (e.g. Boyatzis, 1982). The interest in the UK of Eysenck and Cattell in personality differences, especially in extra-version/introversion and neuroticism, has led to a growth of interest in psychometrically based personality inventories such as the 16PF and more recently Saville and Holdsworth's Occupational Personality Questionnaire. The German Army's apparent success in using situational exercises and simulations in selecting military officers led the War Office Selection Board, and sub-sequently, the Civil Service Selection Board, to also include measurements of actual behaviour under simulated conditions to supplement information obtained from psychometric tests in the form of an 'assessment centre'. Though influential in the UK public service, assessment centre technology did not really begin to be influential in UK industry until re-exported by US-based multinationals in the 1970s. Taken up by Bell Telephone System in 1956, US companies focused assessment centres away from long written case studies and reports and debates on socio-political issues towards shorter, more interactive, more job focused exercises oriented round a set of criteria or 'competencies' deemed essential for job success through prior job analysis. The issue of competencies and their assessment is taken up in Chapter 6.

This model of assessment, with its emphasis on job analysis, techniques such as psychometric tests of ability, personality inventories, situational exercises and simulations, and validation of the effectiveness of selection procedures through criterion-related predictive validity has been very influential in determining research agendas in selection research and in determining models of 'good professional practice', as promulgated on training courses in human resource management and by pro-fessional bodies such as the Institute of Personnel and Develop-ment and the British Psychological Society. However, it has always been less influential in Continental Europe, where more clinical, subjective, holistic and gestalt-influenced perspectives on psychology have held longer sway. This is particularly true of

France and the Latin countries, as is evident for example in the continuing use of graphology and clinical, projective tests such as the Rorschach ink-blot test and the continued importance of the subjective, clinical interview. The tendency in the empiricist Anglo-American tradition has been to disparage these kinds of techniques as unreliable and of poor validity, and to transform them as far as possible into forms that resemble psychometric tests. For example, the recommendation is that the application form be turned into a quantifiable biodata instrument and the interview into a structured inventory.

The principal focus of the psychometric paradigm is the 'job', conceived as a set of discrete tasks. In this model, performance criteria are selected and individual 'attributes' of various kinds (knowledge, skills, abilities, etc.) are chosen as predictors of job performance. The attributes selected are then measured through a variety of procedures (tests, interviews, biodata, etc.) and the assessment process validated primarily in terms of criterion-related predictive validity, usually expressed as a correlation coefficient. Other validity dimensions (e.g. construct, content validity) are also sometimes considered. This model appears to value individualism (individual attributes are taken to predict individual performance), managerialism (the major criteria of performance are the achievement of organizational goals as defined by top management) and utility (cost-benefit analysis of the monetary benefits conferred on organizations in using different selection procedures), though other concerns such as bias or adverse impact on women and minorities are also taken into account (e.g. Herriot 1993). Indeed, recent developments have attempted to give psychologists and personnel practitioners an equal say in the 'language of business' to other business professionals, justifying the investment in human resources in financial terms in the same way that IT specialists may justify the investment in a new IT system or production managers the investment in new operations technologies.

Challenges to the psychometric paradigm

It must first be recognized that this model has a number of considerable strengths, especially in comparison to the kinds of subjective 'gut feel' and prejudiced selection processes that are often used by selectors. Individual differences in performance *do* contribute significantly to differences in organizational performance; even if other factors also affect organizational performance.

In later sections of the book we go on to consider a number of challenges to this dominant paradigm of selection and assessment. From within the paradigm, it has been noted that the model rests on a number of questionable assumptions (e.g. Herriot 1993):

- that people do not change much – assessment characteristics are stable and can be used to predict job performance
- that job content also does not change much, and that job content primarily consists of specific sets of tasks which can be identified through job analysis
- that job performance is measurable in some manner
- that the key purpose of assessment is the prediction of job performance.

As organizations change, decentralize, restructure, get flatter, and devolve accountability, the conception of the 'job' as a stable collection of discrete tasks has come under pressure, and work is no longer packaged in the form of bundles of tasks known as jobs (e.g. Salaman *et al.*, 1992). Multi-skilling, flexible specialization, self-directed work teams and project teams have made this notion of the 'job' rather outdated, and these and other changes such as downsizing and the growth of 'portfolio careers' have changed our concepts of career success and career development. Work no longer comes in job-sized chunks.

Knowledge and skill-based reward systems, performance-related pay systems, cafeteria-based reward systems and 'broad-banding' have also undermined the use of job evaluation and the role of the job as the sole basis for reward systems (e.g. Luthans and Fox, 1989; Armstrong, 1993). Indeed, Bridges (1994) has spoken of 'jobshift' and the rise of the 'jobless society'. Not only has 'employment' declined in the face of the rise of unemployment and the growth of part-time, temporary, sub-contracted and other forms of so-called 'flexible work' such as franchising, tele-working and consultancies, but also in supposedly 'core' jobs much work goes on outside the job matrix, with individuals increasingly selected for career roles rather than jobs, expected to work outside job definitions and even expected to initiate and renegotiate their work roles.

These changes imply that what the psychometric paradigm is attempting to predict – performance in a job – is increasingly becoming fuzzy and ambiguous. Project-based work, with its multiple supervisors, stakeholders and customers, also implies that the use of the traditional criteria of supervisors' assessment of job performance is no longer adequate for the validation of predictors, such as assessment techniques. Turning to alternative criteria such as promotability is not necessarily the answer either. Delayering, downsizing and the decline of the job hierarchy have meant the 'up is not the only way' in career development (e.g. Iles, 1997). Increasingly careers success is being defined in terms of lateral or even downward movements, project work, job enrichment and portfolio careers (Waterman *et al.*, 1994). So the index of promotion success, a major performance criteria used to validate selection effectiveness, is no longer an accurate gauge of work effectiveness.

A more long-standing challenge to this paradigm of assessment has come from political and legal challenges to the fairness and validity of assessment and selection procedures. In the USA in particular, such challenges have come over groups with 'visible differences' such as race, age and gender. Similar concerns, especially with regard to gender but less markedly with regard to age and race have been manifest in recent years in Europe. More recently, sexual orientation has become a major issue in employment. With the rise of the Civil Rights movement and feminism, equal employment opportunity and the avoidance of unfair discrimination have become important social values. Assessment instruments have increasingly come to be criticized as exhibiting unfair and illegal discriminatory features, and the criterion of 'bias' or 'adverse impact' against protected groups has become an increasingly important 'evaluative standard' against which to judge selection procedures.

This situation led to a decline in the use of psychometric tests in the 1970s; it also, however, stimulated research into 'validity generalization' to show that tests *were* in fact valid across situations. In addition, it encouraged research into creating

21

selection procedures which were as valid if not more valid than psychometric tests but which generated less 'adverse impact' against protected groups. Work samples, assessment centres and structured, criteria-related interviews seemed to fit the bill in this respect. All of these procedures display a concern with thorough job analysis to identify the criteria or competencies held to constitute effective job performance and all share a concern to 'sample' job content directly in the selection procedure itself, in the form of simulations of some kind. Hence, there is a rising concern with content validity as well as predictive validity. This in itself marks an interesting departure from the traditional psychometric paradigm, with its concern to assess rather abstract and general 'signs' as predictors. Traditionally, the predictor 'signs', such as abstract personality traits or intellectual abilities, are rather remote from actual measures of a job performance (Wernimont and Campbell, 1967). In the content-oriented 'sample' approach, predictor and criteria measures become as close as possible, both representing 'job performance' in some way. Such procedures not only seem less 'biased' than psychometric tests or traditional unstructured interviews; they also seem of similar or even higher validity, as we shall see in Chapter 3.

Reviewing this whole area shows that the agenda for the psychometric model has not in fact been set by neutral, scientific interests, as often asserted, but by political, social and legal pressures and agendas. More sophisticated, critical adherents to the model (e.g. Hesketh and Robertson, 1993) have called for a clearer conceptual appreciation of the relationships between and among predictors and criteria, and for a better understanding of measurement issues in selection. Their position acknowledges that 'selection has been atheoretical, with a primary focus on identifying approaches and techniques that have practical utility. Comparatively little emphasis has been placed on the development of conceptual frameworks for selection or on trying to understand why some procedures work and others not' (Hesketh and Robertson, 1993: 3). The authors point out that research findings on assessment centres in particular challenge the construct validity of what is being assessed, 'with studies showing that ratings tend to cluster according to exercises rather than in terms of the dimensions being assessed. This question of what is being measured by these attempts to assess job competencies is unresolved and the basis of the validity of such methods is uncertain' (Hesketh and Robinson, 1993: 3).

In recent years this paradigm has also come under fire from other, more fundamentally challenging perspectives. One is rooted in social rather than in differential psychology, and views the assessment process less as a neutral measurement instrument oriented to prediction and more as an interaction or social event with its own rules, expectations and impacts, involving concerns with identity, negotiation and subjectivity. In the US context this paradigm has primarily been influenced by legal, intellectual and political challenges to psychometric model in terms of bias, unfairness and illegal discrimination and by the developing legislation around equal employment opportunity and affirmative action. The research concern here has been primarily to explore the impact of what are often seen in the psychometric model as 'irrelevant' variables, such as race, gender, disability, age, accent and appearance, on assessors' judgements and ratings. In the objective, individualistic and experimental tradition of US social psychology this research has been primarily conducted through experimental studies employing student raters often briefly exposed to 'paper people' rather than real candidates. It also uses résumé extracts, photographs, application forms, simulated appraisals or references, filmed extracts from simulated interviews and extracts from transcripts. This research tradition carries with it all the problems of realism, relevance, artificiality and external validity that such research strategies inevitably raise in general, not just in the selection field (Powell, 1993). In the British context the focus usually has been on field research where 'real-life' managers make 'real' judgements of 'real' candidates (Salaman and Thompson, 1976; Iles, 1990).

This perspective is one we shall term the 'social process' model. Its primary concern is to analyse the often immediate social context assessors use to make judgements, and to show how those judgements are not the outcome of objective, quantifiable processes – the ideal of the psychometric measurement paradigm – but the result of more complex social judgements.

The social process perspective on assessment

This approach contains a number of somewhat disparate elements, which derive from different theoretical and epistemological backgrounds. The common element is the assertion that for a variety of systematic reasons – not just, for example, the competence or commitment of the selector – selectors, in practice, are going to deviate from the prescriptions of the idealized model. In some cases, this deviation is seen as a result of the interplay between selection processes and the nature of the individual. In others, it is seen as normal – a normal outcome of the inflexibility of procedural rules. In the most extreme case, compliance with rules is seen as impossible to achieve or to gauge. All that can be said and all that can be achieved is that those involved somehow manage to demonstrate that they have complied with the rules of procedure. The observer then attempts to make sense of the participants' attempts to make sense of what they are doing when they behave 'rationally', in accordance with what they perceive to be the rules of scientific method as defined by the psychometric paradigm.

In one form, this socio-psychological approach focuses on 'impact' and 'process' and explores the selection process as a social process (e.g. Herriot, 1989). It often examines the impact of selection and assessment processes on candidates (e.g. Iles and Robertson, 1989; Fletcher, 1991; Robertson *et al.*, 1991; de Witte *et al.*, 1992). For example, Iles and Robertson (1989) have presented a theoretical model of the impact of selection and assessment processes on individuals, arguing that both the selection decision and the candidate's attitudes to the selection process are likely to have effects on a variety of psychological processes, including organizational and career attitudes, self-efficacy, self-esteem and other psychological states. These are then likely to lead to such behaviour as job and career withdrawal. Some empirical research in UK banks supports these predictions (Fletcher, 1991; Robertson *et al.*, 1991).

This primarily European-based 'social process' model of assessment makes several assumptions which contrast with those underlying the US-based psychometric model (e.g. Herriot, 1993):

24

- that people change constantly in the course of their careers in organizations
- that subjective self-perceptions are critical to people's work motivation and performance
- that self-perceptions are influenced by assessment selection procedures
- that the jobs people do increasingly involve interaction, negotiation and mutual influence, often taking place in multi-skilled, flexible, self-directed work teams.

Chapter 4 will explore this paradigm and the work conducted within it in more detail and in actual, real organizations as well as in laboratories or classrooms. Often the rather yawning gap between the rhetoric of good selection practice (as defined by the classical paradigm) and the messy, irrational and politically charged reality of actual selection processes is pointed out.

Other forms of this social process approach stress how actual selection processes deviate from the prescribed, idealized psychometric model. In some cases researchers simply stress this divergence, noting that 'recruitment practices are not as sophisticated as the professional model implies: that job descriptions are not widely used; that no explicit evaluation of methods is used; and that firms do have institutionalized methods of recruitment; however these recruitment procedures are normally the product of custom and practice' (Windholf and Wood, 1988: 1). In other cases, the researcher seeks to explain this discrepancy in terms of key organizational processes. Here the focus is less on accounting for the gap between reality and rhetoric, and more on understanding how the rhetoric is used to justify a decision made on grounds other than those allowed for by the formal rules. Salaman and Thompson (1978) for example, argue that the selection of British army officers reveals the use, in practice, of a set of values, understandings and assumptions among selecting officers, distributed among them as part of their shared officer culture. These determine the outcome of selection choices, but are masked by the deployment of, and by the reference to, the formal procedures so that; 'these factors ensure that an inevitable residue of flexible *ad hoc* practices, within the otherwise scientific selection process undermines the scientificity (objectivity and universalism) of the evaluations while maintaining the "scientific charter"' (Salaman and Thompson, 1978: 303).

A more radical version of this model focuses on the processes whereby selection systems, processes, decisions, discussions are managed so that they can be presented (and indeed experienced) as rational. This approach is also concerned with the rationality of decisions – not in the sense that it supports the possibility of a neutral, objective process of decision making which produces a true analysis of the candidate (the psychometric model), but in the sense that it focuses on how selectors have to behave in order to persuade themselves and others that their decisions and process are reasonable and in accordance with the proper procedures. In this perspective, an account of any reality – in our case, an account of a selection candidate in terms of psychological dimensions and psychometric techniques – derives its rationality not from its direct correspondence with the objective world, but from the ability of those involved in the decision to make sense of the account and to demonstrate its sense to others (Silverman and Jones, 1973, 1976). A further development of this model, which we shall term the discourse approach, is treated in more detail in Chapter 5, but is outlined here.

A discourse perspective

This approach focuses on the ways in which an area of activity, study or attention is constructed, known and measured. It regards psychometric psychology, for example, as a form of discourse; an authoritative way of knowing something – in this case employees, or would-be employees. Drawing heavily on the work of Michel Foucault, Miller and Rose (1993: 79) define a discourse as 'a technology of thought, requiring attention to the particular technical devices of writing, listing, numbering and computing that render a realm into discourse as a knowable, calculable and administrative object'. 'Knowing' an object in such a way that it can be governed is more than a purely speculative activity: it requires the invention of procedures of notation, ways of collecting and presenting statistics, the transportation of these to centre where calculations and judgements can be made. This approach clearly offers a distinctive view of the selection process. The identification of employee attributes or management competencies and the technology of the assessment of these competencies is now conceptualized as an instance of the 'knowing' and constituting of individuals as employees or managers. The psychometric discourse is here seen as consisting of a complex set of intellectual, science-based conceptual frameworks allied to psychologically and psychometrically based technology for the identification and assessment and (crucially) measurement of individuals against defined criteria.

The discourse approach argues that psychometrics constitutes an example of the discursive practice whereby objects – in this case individuals – are known and constructed as employees through forms of discourse, whereby their meaning is defined. Their truth claims are dependent not on their objective correspondence with the 'real world' (for all worlds are discursively constructed) but fundamentally on power relations.

Selection and assessment processes in this model can be seen not in terms of their efficiency, or reasonableness, or even in terms of the ways in which such reasonableness is constructed and displayed (as in the social process model) but in terms of the relationships between these processes, the expertise on which they are based, and the practice of power within organizations. So far all the perspectives on assessment and selection discussed (the strategic, the psychometric and the social process) take efficiency as their prime concern; they focus on ways of improving the efficiency of the process or seek to explain current developments in selection procedures and criteria terms of change in the nature of work organizations. In the discourse perspective, selection and current developments in the identification of competencies may be regarded as elements in the 'government' or regulation of organizations and employees.

The discourse approach addresses the ways in which, power, knowledge and practice mutually support and reproduce each other. This approach does not simply argue that practices and knowledge support power in an ideological or legitimating manner, as found in many Marxist accounts of selection technologies. Instead, it argues that power is that 'which transverses *all* practices – from the 'macro' to the 'micro' – through which persons are ruled, mastered, held in check, administered, steered, guided, by means of which they are led by others or have come to direct or regulate their own actions' (Rose, 1990). Power is thus not located merely in the actions of the State or within the enterprise in the actions of senior managers; it is seen as present in *all* knowledges and practices that regulate individuals, including of course their own self-regulation. Thus this approach allows us to look for the exercise or practice of power in activity which initially may seem far removed from established centres of power, such as the Government, the Chief Executive Officer, or the Board, or removed through the nature and exercise of scientific expertise from direct attribution to the interests and values of the powerful. The process of selection is therefore seen in this perspective as a clear example of the exercise of power within the detached and scientific process of psychometric or competence-based assessment (Hollway, 1991).

Power is here seen as inherent in knowledge itself, and in the techniques which that knowledge informs and justifies. Knowledge, as the analysis of competencies and the assessment processes reveals, comes to play a major role in constructing the individual employee as someone calculable, discussable and capable of being comprehended in the process of, and as the subject of, senior managerial interventions and decisions. The process of selection and assessment is therefore one key site for such construction and such intervention; it is fundamentally seen as a site of organizational government.

Miller and Rose have made the point that, following Foucault, the term 'government' can usefully be employed to focus on 'the shifting ambitions and concerns of all those social authorities that have sought to administer the lives of individuals and associations, focusing our attention on the diverse mechanisms through which the actions and judgements of persons and organisations have been linked to political objectives' (Miller and Rose, 1993: 75–6). These authors argue that this project is greatly enhanced by a further concept (that of 'governmentality'), used to draw attention to the diverse and various processes and techniques under discussion. They quote Foucault in defining this concept: 'an ensemble formed by the institutions, procedures, analyses and reflections, the calculations and tactics, that allow the exercise of this very specific albeit complex form of power' (Foucault,

1974: 20, quoted in Miller and Rose, 1993: 76). The processes of selection and assessment are here seen as offering a striking example of a major way in which selectors' actions and judgements on candidates (internal decisions in assessment for promotion, development or deselection, external decisions in selection), critical for organizational restructuring and for individual experience, are structured and made rational in terms of expert-derived systems and criteria of selection.

From this perspective, processes of assessment and selection are seen as revealing the interrelationships between knowledge and power, demonstrating the ubiquity and diversity of power/knowledge practices and showing the role of a form of organizational governmentality which allows the exercise of power through calculation, assessment and knowledge. Processes of selection and assessment, wherein individuals and employees are 'known' in terms of a set of qualities, measured against these, and processed in terms of this assessment, are therefore seen as at least as revealing of organizations as they are of individuals.

Recent developments in, and applications of, discourse theory therefore represent far more than the pursuit of academic relativism. Studying established scientific practice, such as processes and procedures of scientific selection and assessment in terms of discourse theory, may offer an invaluable opportunity to view these important practices in terms other that those in which they present themselves. It enables us to see these activities not only in terms of their construction and measurement of job-relevant qualities, of inscribing dimensions of individuals so that they can be described, assessed, compared and processed, but also in terms of the expert management of subjectivity – the production, distribution and utilization of truths about individuals that define them in terms that make them knowable and usable. This knowledge is part of wider processes and techniques that dominate the ways in which, within organizations, members relate to each other, and even to themselves. The power and pervasiveness of the discourse of the psychometric paradigm in particular and the classical model of assessment in general makes its questioning both more necessary and more difficult. This is a project which is in its very early stages.

2

A STRATEGIC MANAGEMENT PERSPECTIVE

———————

Accompanying the rise in influence of human resource management approaches to employee relations has come an increasing emphasis on the strategic management of assessment. In the introduction, it was pointed out that assessment programmes will need to be integrated with other human resource management (HRM) programmes and activities, as decisions taken in one HR area will clearly have implications for other areas, with specific implications for the design of jobs and for the kinds of skills and attributes needed to do those jobs. This has immediate implications for the type of assessment procedures needed, as well as for the numbers and kinds of people required by the organization. This is not, however, often taken into account in most models of assessment. The strategic management approach argues that organizations will need to engage in human resource planning if they are to be able to forecast assessment needs and the likely availability of staff, both externally and internally. Such human resource planning will need to be strategic and flexible, and can be used to identify recruitment needs. There is no point in estimating, for example, how many graduates an organization will need to recruit before deciding on what it wants graduates *for*. This requires close attention to what skills the organization feels it needs for various categories of staff, both immediately and in the future. Such forecasts are likely to be influenced by the strategic direction taken by the organization, and are rarely made in practice, except by some large, sophisticated organizations.

For example, redefinition of the organization's structure, culture or mission may require the specification of new skills and competencies and the identification of people, both internally and externally, who possess these qualities. Strategic realignment may also influence career paths and expectations, perhaps generating uncertainty and disappointment. Existing values and ways of doing things may no longer seem sufficient. Changes in culture and values may affect the organization's recruitment image and its ability to recruit and hire the people it needs. Alternatively, new opportunities for internal staff may open up, and new career paths may be generated. Changes to both employment contracts and what is often termed the 'psychological contract' between employee and organization are likely. Box 2.1 discusses some developments of this kind in the UK financial services industry.

The UK IT industry has also exhibited a more strategic approach to assessment and selection, and has witnessed profound changes with significant implications for assessment processes. Many IT companies neglected the long-term planning of recruitment, selection and training due to their perceived need to meet immediate technical needs and work pressures. Though manufacturing and other industries had begun spending less strongly on data processing in the 1980s, the communications, retail and financial sectors were still buoyant, with IT becoming a key to competitive advantage in many sectors. Purchasers were also becoming more sophisticated, needing specialized software. This required a more strategic relationship between user and supplier. Competitive restructuring, price wars, falling profit margins, strategic partnerships to reduce R & D costs, technology sharing agreements, takeovers and amalgamation have also been common in this industry.

An increasing proportion of revenue has come from consultancy training, software applications and maintenance and a focus on 'total service', which relies more on high quality, skilled people. This emphasis on service quality requires the acquisition and development of people with new technical and managerial

Box 2.1

Building societies in the UK have developed over the years from the bonding together of factory workers into mutual clubs. The term 'mutual' is still used by some societies, as is the term 'permanent'. This illustrates the roots of building societies as having a kind of social purpose. It was common in the 1980s to speak of the 'building societies movement', of societies having 'members' rather than 'customers', and of generating 'surpluses' not 'profits'.

The Building Societies Act 1986 removed building societies from the traditional cartel and pushed them into a more competitive environment. Some societies moved into estate agency, the provision of travellers cheques and the offering of different types of loans. The Financial Services Act 1987, embodying as it does the principle of 'polarization', caused societies to re-examine the role of insurance and whether to be independent themselves (for example, the Halifax) or whether to represent insurance companies.

The Abbey National for instance, in the late 1980s sought to demutualize, moving to public limited company (plc) status and, to all intents and purposes, become a bank. Other societies, such as the Bradford and Bingley, have sought to preserve their 'social movement/community service' aura as a differentiator, as opposed to the stereotyped large, bureaucratic, profit-oriented, cold, impersonal bank. In the 1990s, many other societies (e.g. the Halifax, Northern Rock, the Woolwich) have taken the Abbey National path.

In the 1990s, the business strategy of the National and Provincial Building Society was to be a major provider of personal financial services in four distinct areas: savings, mortgages, insurance, consumer credit (personal loans and credit cards).

The Society believed that the key to coping with the speed of change was an integrated human resource strategy (HRS). This meant that it needed to identify what skills and competencies would be needed in the future, and to define its jobs in terms of current and future skill requirements. This strategy requires the continuous auditing and profiling of prospective and existing staff and the introduction of development programmes which can assist employees in upgrading and enhancing their skills. This is closely linked to a set of new core values fundamental to realizing the strategy: 'accountability', 'customer care', 'enterprise', 'success' – ACES.

In 1988, the National and Provincial decided that a business-driven human resource development (HRD) strategy was a necessary response to the challenges it faced. Management Development in particular was accepted as a corporate activity crucial in sustaining core values in an increasingly diversified organization. The society felt that effective HRD required the commitment of business managers, not just human resource management specialists, and that successful HRD needed to be an integral part of the business policy and planning process, delivering present and future business objectives. This required knowledge of business plans and an understanding of the managerial competencies required to meet changing needs.

A number of initiatives were introduced:

1 Closer linkage of 'off-the-job' development activities with relevant work objectives and activities.
2 Tighter links between corporate business objectives and individual performance objectives.
3 The introduction of business-driven development into performance reviews, with measurable objectives.
4 Regular review of objectives and individual performance, in addition to annual appraisal.
5 Making all managers accountable for staff development.
6 Establishing a separate training function, National and Provincial Training Services, operating as a separate business offering competence-based internal programmes to National and Provincial businesses. These programmes were to emphasize tailor-made packages rather than standard programmes to reflect the different needs of different businesses.
7 Sponsorship of managers on MBA and DBA programmes at Lancaster and Bradford Universities.
8 The establishment of a Group Management Development Unit, concerned with strategic managerial needs and separate from training.
9 Use of external development opportunities to give breadth, including the assembly of a training database.
10 The closer alignment of individual performance appraisal and corporate business activity.

One key element in their approach was to develop key post competencies and to identify and develop a pool of managers with the potential to compete for these posts, rather than to plan succession to individual posts. These competencies were used to asses, select and develop future managers and were weighted in favour of strategically important key skills. Since National and Provincial also felt that any competence framework needed to be both 'owned' by the staff and reflective of the future desired culture, it rejected 'off-the-shelf' solutions derived in different businesses and cultures and decided to develop its own competence model. This involved getting senior managers to define those competencies required for each key post in behavioural terms, using critical incident interviews with key post-holders and their bosses.

The key method of profiling people against the required competencies was to use assessment and development centres. Participants were nominated by managers through a fairly intensive screening process, so that the managers and the participants in centres were actually aware of its implications and consequences.

Each assessor saw each candidate, and the candidates were seen under a variety of circumstances. Assessors tried to come to some kind of agreed rating or a score for the candidates, and then to go beyond that to identify their strengths and weaknesses, to explore development needs and opportunities and identify options for development.

The initiatives were held together through a Personal Development Plan. Participants in the development centre had a discussion with their manager about their competency in relation to the current job and their competency in relation to future roles, so as to identify development needs.

National and Provincial also used the competencies in other parts of their HR operation:

1 *Recruitment:* Job specifications covering not only major accountabilities but also key competencies were produced for all posts.
2 *Selection:* A variety of selection procedures were used to explore applicant competencies.
3 *Promotion:* This was based increasingly on business performance and the competencies required in the new role, with planned personal development programmes to bridge gaps.

Despite the integration of human resource strategies with the overall corporate strategy, National and Provincial did not perform as

34

well as expected and this resulted in a change of Chief Executive and the development of a new way forward, still based firmly on a competence approach.

The 'old' corporate strategy had generated several problems; for example, in its drive to acquire new financial service capabilities, the society pursued an acquisition route that carried within it the seeds of conflict between old and new businesses. These conflicts were exacerbated by the geographic divide. Most of the old 'core' business was located in the North of England, the new in the South.

The competence-driven HR strategy was seen as a positive step forward and competence profiles for all jobs, not just key posts, were developed. All staff could have their competence levels assessed and, as a consequence, the elitist approach to management development associated with the previous strategy was abandoned. Cultural values were reoriented around 'advice and guidance' and around developing relationships with customers, rather than just selling products. This changed the way that competencies were expressed in behavioural terms. National and Provincial subsequently merged with the Abbey National.

(*Source:* Iles, 1992; Mabey and Iles, 1993)

---

skills, such as process, communication, leadership, entrepreneurial, project management and people management skills. Recruitment has continued to be a major HRM activity, while skills shortages have continued. There is still often a preference for recruiting experienced people and graduates. Graduate recruitment has been increasing, and suppliers have looked to widen their net to identify people with potential. There has been increasing use of psychometric assessment, such as tests of verbal and numerical ability. Broadening recruitment to non-computer science graduates has also reinforced the strategy of selling *business* solutions, not technological ones. People have tended to be recruited for experience and paid to perform. High attrition rates, little loyalty and a reluctance to train have resulted. Most suppliers have used high rewards to fend off skills shortages, a strategy problematic for smaller companies and one that has back-fired on larger companies. Financial companies, for example, have also paid well for experienced IT staff. Marketing functions have grown in importance as compared to sales and engineering, bringing in people with different skills to maintain customer relationships, cultural conflicts, an emphasis on managing culture to create congruent goals, beliefs and attitudes, a shift towards developing people, and an emphasis on improving customer relationships and managerial processes. Skills shortages have stimulated a greater focus on development, especially cross-functional development and transfers from technical support and engineering to sales. Third-party maintenance, the recruitment of young, less skilled engineers to maintain the high volume end of the market and a greater use of contract staff and networking have also increased in frequency. Multi-skilling people does not always work, however, as engineers, support people and sales staff all have different work attitudes. It is often difficult to develop sales staff into support people, for example, or vice versa.

Most IT departments of UK companies still see a need for graduates, despite reduced supply and increasing competition. Many departments have responded to these challenges by including ex-graduates on interview boards to increase their acceptability, by drawing on a wider pool of subject areas, by using more psychometric techniques, by using more centralized graduate recruitment programmes, by recruiting more female staff, and by moves into international graduate recruitment. However, such programmes are only feasible for large departments and leave untapped the wide potential available among non-graduates (Sparrow *et al.*, 1989).

For example, the major electronics and communications company ICL (now owned by Fujitsu) has made extensive use of psychometric testing and psychological assessment in recruitment, training, career development, counselling and team building. These programmes were integrated into an overall human resource strategy (linked with business strategy) and presented in a consistent, standardized way.

Both the companies STC and ICL had made extensive use of psychometric testing and psychological assessment in recruitment, training, career development, counselling and team building in the 1980s. ICL sought to integrate these into an overall human resources strategy. A major concern was to ensure a consistent, standardized approach worldwide, with an Organization and Management Review used to bind the processes together. Psychometric tests of ability and personality were used, alongside one-to-one interviews. The tests used were not generic ones but exclusive to ICL, as was the competence language employed. Tests and assessment centres were used at major career points as a way of reducing loss and recruitment costs and as a way of extending the base for management development and succession. These points were after two to three years of graduate entry, after five to six years and after 10 to 15 years. Graduates were not divided at entry into those who were high fliers and those who were not; division into technical specialists and general managers occurred after substantial work experience. A general assessment of business general management potential was made between the ages of 28 and 35, with key individuals being developed at these points. Organizational Management Reviews used career profiles to summarize key capabilities, growth potential, career direction, career aiming points, development needs and appropriate action plans. Assessment centres were used in the form of 'career guidance centres' at all stages; for the participants aged 28 to 35 they were used against general management criteria. An interesting feature of this procedure is that it employed board directors as assessors, and these continued to act as future mentors (Jones, 1990).

This example shows a company employing a rigorous, standardized set of assessment procedures, including psychometric tests and assessment centres, employed at various career stages. Particularly strong features are the desire to integrate assessment into other HRM activities and the desire to integrate people management into business strategy. The company seems to use an organization-specific set of competencies as criteria and similarly specific set of psychometric tests. This may ensure greater commitment and ownership of the process and greater acceptance of the language used in the assessment procedures; presumably these tests reflect organizational realities more fully than 'generic' tests. However, there is no indication of the predictive validity of the tests; the company will need to undertake its own validation exercises, and this may prove prohibitive for small companies. It is also difficult using this approach to compare company managers with other managers in the sector. Moreover, the system is also elitist, favouring high potential managers only and focused on graduates recruited in their early twenties. A standardized approach may also incur costs in terms of a loss of flexibility and may generate problems in matching assessment and selection strategies to the needs of particular businesses, business units or product life cycles. However, it may ensure quality control over which consultants and which tests are employed.

In central and local government in the UK a similar review of assessment and selection procedures has taken place. The formation of the Employment Service into an agency, for example, prompted it to demand more control over the Executive Officer Selection process, devolving it to local management. Key targets for the system included speeding up the recruitment cycle, controlling costs and establishing a system that was valid, reliable, acceptable to the Treasury and with high face validity so that the people using the system would want to use it. In addition, it had to attract a wider range of applicants, including older people, people with disabilities and minority ethnic groups. It still needed to assess for skills and competencies required across the Employment Department Group as a whole, not just within the Agency, so as to permit transfer and open up career paths. Analysis of the required competencies through documents, interviews and focus groups was followed by the development of selection methods and work samples. At all stages user involvement was ensured through consultation with relevant groups within the Employment Service (Kandola and Cross, 1992).

Having illustrated the way several leading companies have introduced a more strategic approach to the way they manage staff selection and assessment, we need to explore the ways assessment processes seem often to be related to several dimensions associated with corporate strategy such as:

- organizational design and structure
- business life cycles
- corporate strategy and product-market strategies.

We will next explore the assessment implications in relation to each of these dimensions.

Organizational design, structure and assessment

Different organizational configurations seem to require different skills and characteristics, and therefore different assessment criteria.

Functional designs

In functional designs the organization is divided into groups performing specialized functions, providing a clear, visible and well-understood ladder of promotion, advancement and career development. This tends to foster a functional culture of high cohesiveness. However, it may discourage a wider view, flexibility or integration, and may tend to encourage rigid promotion practices within functional specialisms. Such narrow experience and development may not lead to visionary general managers. Functional designs may also tend to isolate assessment processes from strategic concerns, unless cross-functional development programmes are instituted. Managers may be very well qualified for technical projects but less well equipped for change, ambiguity, or taking a corporate rather than functional perspective.

Divisional designs

In divisional designs functions are combined into product, client, customer, or area groups, and members are defined by their relationship to these groups rather than by specialization. Such a design should stimulate synergy and the development of generalists, as strategic decisions need to be taken at much earlier career stages compared to functional organizations. A broader perspective is required, which means that a different set of experiences, skills and criteria for promotion needs to be developed and applied to assessment processes, not just specialist expertise. For example, a good R & D manager may exhibit quite different characteristics from a good research scientist.

Such a design may, however, stimulate conflicts over scarce resources between relatively autonomous groups and create ambiguity over promotion ladders and career development.

Some jobs may seem like stepping stones, others like dead ends; some positions may lead to exposure, visibility and political influence, others may be the equivalent of running a power station in Siberia.

Matrix forms

Matrix forms attempt to build on the strengths and avoid the weaknesses of both of the other forms. They seem particularly appropriate in responding to rapid change. Successful performance here calls for both specialism and breadth, and the simultaneous coordination of both functional and product requirements. It allows the early identification of a manager's potential and the provision of early strategic experiences, but may also generate frustration and instability. People may be continually working with multiple bosses and on multiple, time-limited projects, which may prove stressful.

However, it is not just at the managerial level that assessment criteria have changed. In recent years many British and European companies have sought to move from low technology, labour intensive manufacturing processes to high technology, computer-integrated processes. This has required greater employee flexibility. For recruitment, selection and development purposes the new requirements needs to be specified, including the nature of the new culture and structure and the specific behaviours that will be needed. This has often necessitated a thorough job analysis to identify the kinds of skills necessary for effective present and future performance. Moves from a stable, product-driven culture to a more dynamic, market-driven one, and moves from a hierarchical, individualistic, demarcated structure with closely supervised, restricted jobs towards a flatter, more team based, more flexible structure with more autonomy and a reliance on self-monitoring may also require new selection and assessment criteria. These might include openness to new ideas, adaptability, a desire to improve, an ability to see multiple perspectives, broad vision, an ability to visualize relationships, a tolerance of uncertainty, a readiness to accept responsibility, self-confidence, a liking for change, and greater team-working skills (Pearn and Kandola, 1992).

Business life cycles and assessment processes

Organizational strategies for managing various businesses may also influence assessment strategies, as different criteria are important in different types of business at different stages of growth. Organizations using a portfolio approach may try to develop a differentiated approach to assessment. For example, if an organization plans to divest and withdraw from a particular business, particular skills, experiences and qualities may be needed to manage it. It may be tempting to assign plateaued or superfluous managers to such a business, but employee morale and commitment and customer/client goodwill will need to be monitored and costs controlled. This may require a highly skilled manager who will need reassurance on his or her career back in the organization after divestiture.

Most attention in this area has been paid in the notion of *matching managers to strategies*. This in part is a rejection of the universalistic, generalist notion of managerial skills, whereby a good manager is supposed to be able to manage any organization. This view, in contrast, suggests that emphasis should be given to selecting managers whose skills, styles and competencies 'fit' the requirements of specific strategies. Managers required to manage businesses moving from a 'defend' strategy to divestment, or from growth to maturity, may need to manifest quite different behaviours. Quite different actions may need to be taken with regard to resource allocation, product/market position and investment practices.

It is often asserted that different kinds of managers will need to be recruited and selected to implement different strategies. However, the general strategies (explosive growth, steady state, etc.) are not often translated into specific job requirements and behaviours, leaving the kind of skills, experience, characteristics or competencies required of the managers rather vaguely defined. What kinds of manager needed are usually described only in terms of the functional skills necessary to implement the strategy, or in terms of rather broadly based 'personality' factors.

It should be noted that it is probably over simple to suggest that one should always aim solely at matching managers and strategy.

41

It might be asserted that building up a 'question mark' business will need a manager who is entrepreneurial, proactive and willing to take risks. However, such a manager might also need skills in planning, coordination and cost control. More attention needs to be given to analysis of the position, requirements, the future of the job, and where it is going. Strategic direction may be an important consideration in making an assessment decision, but many other business factors will determine the specifications for the position and the kind of individual required. Attention will also need to be given to the whole management team, not just the individual general manager.

However, it could be argued that it is necessary to be much more specific about the kinds of managerial skills and characteristics needed to make businesses successful in different business situations. As the environment changes, so must the necessary set of competencies. Some people are better at starting things up, others at closing them down. By analysing the jobs systematically, and by collecting behavioural data on managers in a systematic way, it may be possible to be much more rigorous in relating selection and placement decisions to the job requirements of a chosen strategy. This may require:

1 The specification of strategy-related job requirements, in terms of a future-oriented job description.
2 The specification of dimensions of managerial effectiveness, in terms of future-oriented person specifications.
3 The use of a set of systematic assessment techniques, such as assessment centres and criterion-based interviewing techniques.

One approach to identifying the characteristics required by candidates in positions associated with specific strategies, developed by Gerstein and Reisman (1983), utilizes the following dimensions of senior managerial competence and effectiveness:

1 *Problem solving:*
  • problem identification and analysis
  • solution implementation

2 *Administration:*
- execution and control
- communication
- delegation
- crisis management
- negotiation

3 *HRM:*
- strategic integration
- assessment
- development
- strategy formulation
- openness to innovation and change

4 *Organizational leadership:*
- interpersonal empathy and influence
- group management skills
- helicopter vision
- self-motivation
- emotional strength and maturity
- personal integrity
- general management knowledge.

These competencies are assessed through two assessment techniques, both of which we shall explore in more detail later in the book.

1 behavioural interviewing
2 assessment centres.

Information from these two sources is then combined with an assessment of technical capabilities and personality characteristics.

In summary, this life-cycle model of strategic assessment (Woodruffe, 1990) involves:

1 specification of business situation and strategic direction
2 confirmation or modification of organizational structure
3 development of role descriptions for key jobs, including existing jobs
4 assessment of key personnel in the management team

5 matching of individuals and positions, with attention to team balance

6 implementing the changes in a planned manner.

Assessment strategies and product-market strategies

Assessment policies, it is often argued, should involve a strategic response to business conditions in order to accomplish distinct missions. Two useful approaches to corporate strategy and its relationship to assessment strategies are presented by Miles and Snow (1984) and Porter (1980). This section will explore the assessment and selection implications of such frameworks, following Herriot (1992).

Miles and Snow – strategic types

These authors identify four strategic types of firms – prospectors, defenders, analysers and reactors – according to how they adapt to their environment, and outline specific assessment requirements for each type. In the next section we will elaborate on these suggestions, using the dimensions 'assignment flow' and 'supply flow'.

Prospectors
Prospector firms seek to locate and exploit new opportunities, develop new products and create new markets. Internal efficiency is seen as less important than innovation, and core skills tend to lie in marketing and/or R & D. These firms tend to have a diverse product line and multiple technologies. Their assessment systems must therefore attempt to locate technical experts who are creative and independent.

Defenders
Defenders tend to be 'core firms' within a narrow product/ market domain, seeking to protect that domain through efficient production, strong control mechanisms, and continuity and reliability. Core skills are often in finance and/or production.

Defenders tend to have limited product lines, single capital intensive technology and a functional structure. Their assessment systems must therefore seek to find and produce long-term loyal members high in commitment to the organization.

Analysers

Analysers fall between these two groups, taking fewer risks than prospectors but excelling in the delivery of new products and service. They tend to rapidly adopt promising ideas, have a limited product line, and search for a small number of fruitful opportunities. Often with matrix structures, their core skills tend to be marketing, process engineering and production efficiency. Their assessment systems need to recruit and develop people who take moderate risks but also remain loyal to the organization.

Reactors

Reactors are firms with little control over their environment and indeed may be buffeted by it. They lack control over vital resources or may lack the ability to adapt to external competition. There is often misalignment between strategy and environment, or between strategy, process and structure. Their assessment systems must seek to dispense with staff through lay-offs, discharges, early retirements and out-placements, with limited recruitment of 'turnaround' experts.

Each strategic type seems to be associated with a particular HR orientation and particular HR practices, including assessment practices. Prospectors with a divisional structure tend to have a strategy of *acquiring* human resources and an emphasis on recruitment and selection, performance based rewards and job rotation. Defenders with functional structures tend towards a strategy of *building* human resources through recruitment, selection, training and socialization. Analysers tend to combine elements of both systems, smaller analysers using functional structures and larger analysers creating semi-autonomous divisions for diversification and matrix structures for handling innovations. They tend to be interested in *allocating* human resources, using planned interdivisional transfers, career planning, OD (organizational development), job design, team building, assessment centres, and lateral movement of people with scarce technical skills. Defenders tend to be low-cost producers, prospectors, product differentiators, and analysers focused operators in niche markets, to use the Porter (1980) terminology.

European examples of defenders might include the former British Rail, British Coal or perhaps Littlewoods or Tate and Lyle; that is, organizations which try to seal off a market segment and dominate it. Many public sector organizations fall into this category, although the situation is changing under the impact of privatization, competitive tendering, deregulation and local management of schools. Examples of prospectors might include Hanson or BAT, while IBM or Shell would count as analysers. Many organizations have been forced into reactor mode under the influence of the recessions of the 1980s and 1990s. Many companies in the manufacturing sector, in the textile industry particularly, seem to fall into this category, as well as organizations in the retail and hotel sectors.

For example, in the eighteenth and nineteenth centuries, the British textile industry was characterized by prospector-like innovation strategies – the Aire and Calder valleys seem to have been the Silicon Valleys of the 1790s! Textile firms became stable, secure and defender-like in the early twentieth century, only to be exposed to the turbulent winds of recession in the 1970s. Many sought more innovative, customer-oriented and flexible responses in the 1980s, but despite product diversification few show prospector characteristics. Some have succeeded in surviving and prospering, in terms of product volume and value if not in levels of employment.

This industry illustrates that the above classification does not describe a static, unchanging picture. Many British and European organizations have attempted to shift from one mode to another as environmental circumstances have changed (Herriot, 1992). Frequent shifts have taken place in the 1990s, as described below.

- *From defender to reactor*: Many firms, buffeted by the 1980s recessions, have been forced into reactor mode. The UK textile industry shows many examples, as does the building society industry.
- *From defender to analyser*: Many private sector defenders in the

UK have found that they cannot remain competitive merely by being more efficient; increased competition may require more innovation. Many financial service organizations have had to innovate and diversify under the impact of deregulation and political, social and technological change. Many have sought to retain their core products or services – for example, building societies have continued to offer savings and mortgage facilities. They have also sought to enter new markets, such as personal credit, insurance and estate agency, or travel and financial planning services.

Some public sector organizations have attempted to make this shift, especially under the impact of government legislation. This includes the impact of privatization on the former state utilities; the impact of competitive tendering legislation and local management of schools on local authorities; the impact of agency status on central governmental departments; the impact of contracting out; and the introduction of quasi-markets in the National Health Service.

- *From defender to prospector*: Some defenders have engaged in a strategy of rapid diversification into new markets through the acquisition of other businesses. Few, however, have tried to shift organically through increased expenditure on research and development.

- *From analyser to prospector*: Some analysers have realized that their innovation and entrepreneurial activity have been inhibited by centralized decision making and have sought to decentralize into small prospector organizations.

- *From prospector to analyser*: Some prospectors – for example, some small, high-technology organizations such as Silicon Graphics, a fast-growing computer systems company in Theale, Berkshire – have sought to become more like analysers as they have grown and developed.

Aligning corporate strategy with assessment practice

In the previous section, we presented one analysis of strategic types, developed by Miles and Snow (1984). Here, we present a more thorough analysis of the relationship between strategic type and assessment practice, based on Sonnenfeld and Peiperl (1988) and Herriot (1992) and using two dimensions: supply flow and assignment flow. Each strategic type of organization seems to operate a different kind of assessment strategy depending on:

1 *Supply flow*: The openness of the assessment system to the external labour market at other than entry levels. Advertising, broadcasting and entertainment firms have extensive mid-career recruitment, outside supply, and mid-career exit. The choice here is essentially between internal and external recruitment.

2 *Assignment flow*: This relates to the criteria by which placement and promotion decisions are made, especially whether they are made on the basis of individual performance or group contribution.

These two dimensions can be used to generate a four-cell typology showing the entry, placement and exit assessment characteristics of four types of firms (Herriot, 1992): baseball teams, academies, clubs and fortresses.

Baseball teams

Baseball teams rely on skills and talents that can be taken to other teams via scouts and agents. They are open to the external labour market at all levels, assigning and promoting individuals on the basis of individual merit. There is continued pressure for creativity and performance, with primarily calculative involvement by members. Consultancy firms, law firms, executive search firms, investment banks, advertising, public relation firms, and broadcasting and entertainment firms may fall into this category. They emphasize recruitment, on the job development and turnover. Career moves mainly happen *between* organizations. As prospectors, they tend to make rapid movements into new markets and attempt to attract 'stars', perhaps to turn around reactors or fortresses. Examples also include conglomerates like BAT or Hanson.

48

Academies
Academy firms try to develop member's knowledge, skills and commitment, while rewarding individual performance. They tend to promote from within, being relatively closed to outside labour markets. They are often dominant or core competitors, fostering professional growth, teamwork, lateral career paths, early career progression, dual career ladders, and limited functional identification. They seek to develop and retain talent, and emphasize firm-specific knowledge and related job sequences. Such types are often found in electronics, automobiles, pharmaceutical and office product sectors. IBM is a classic example, at least until the 1980s. Characteristically analysers, they are not necessarily at the leading technological edge but are careful in their entry to new markets or products. They need both specialist expertise and wide business knowledge, with rapid promotion of 'stars'. Other examples include M & S, Shell, BP and ICI.

Clubs
Clubs tend to emphasize fair treatment, loyalty and seniority. While also using an internal supply of labour, they may focus more attention on group factors. They also emphasize educational qualifications, and are often shielded by regulations or monopoly situations. They may also see themselves as having a 'mission', such as 'public service' or 'Community'. Banks before 1980, airlines, the military, government agencies, British Telecom before privatization, utilities and museums may come into this category, as might the UK Civil Service before the establishment of 'Next Steps' agencies and the introduction of market testing and other market mechanisms (e.g. the Royal Mail). Under the impact of deregulation, many clubs have sought to become more like academies.

Fortresses
Under the impact of competition, many clubs and academies may become fortresses. These are organizations under siege, seeking survival through retrenchment and lay-offs with limited commitment from members. Some firms may go through a 'fortress' phase as a planned transition towards a more baseball-team like structure after streamlining (e.g. advertising, films, banks).

Others may remain in this category for a long time. Textile firms, publishing, hotels, retail organizations and mail order firms may resemble fortresses. They may buy in new top management teams (e.g. the Littlewoods Organization has recruited top managers from ICI, Cable and Wireless, and WH Smith in recent years) and also use cheap labour. Many reactor fortresses may become so under the impact of recession or competition.

This model emphasizes that different management practices within each assessment system are often a product of different strategic intentions. An 'analyser' strategy may require innovation by technical experts. An associated 'academy' career system may demand a careful inventory of internal resources to offer better quality solutions rather than totally innovative ones. 'Prospectors' may attract cosmopolitan, innovative talent committed more to their occupation or profession than to their firm, with baseball-team emphasis on the acquisition of talent at all levels and high performance. 'Defenders' may have a more 'club' like system, often with regulatory and community support and with a 'public service' ethos of benevolence and paternalism. 'Reactors' may have failed at their mission, be in a transitional mode, or be in a sector where such a stance is common.

One might expect senior managers at academies and clubs to have spent a long time in their firms due to their 'closed' assessment systems, in contrast to those at fortresses and baseball teams. Rates of turnover at clubs and academies would be relatively low also, while baseball teams may encourage more job moves. Academies and clubs may generate long-term commitment through career management, reward strategies, and training and development programmes. Clubs are more likely to create generalists, academies functional specialists.

Individuals entering clubs will probably be interested in security, while those entering baseball teams will be more risk taking and interested in advancement, not necessarily within the firm. Commitment to the organization is likely to be higher in clubs, commitment to the career or profession higher in baseball teams. Those entering academies may be more likely to be interested in longer-term rewards and to be committed to their organization. Those entering fortresses may have done so before they became that way, because of a strong interest in or commitment to the organization, because they see few opportunities elsewhere, or because they foresee major sacrifices and disruptions if they leave.

Many firms may have the attributes of more than one career system, especially firms that have very diverse functions or conglomerates with separate business units. Academies are most likely to have only one assessment system, due to their fostering of a strong cultural identity. Many firms may change assessment systems over time as they develop new strategies or lines of business or as the external environment changes. Many organizations like building societies in the UK are trying to move from being a club to being an academy; others are trying to become baseball teams, while many baseball teams are trying to recruit stars from academies. Many academies are trying to keep their stars through career planning and rapid promotion (e.g. old universities offering personal chairs to stop new universities from poaching star performers).

The value of this analysis is that it questions the frequent assumption that organizations need to display a common set of values and assumptions. It is often assumed that internal promotion and development and extensive training and employment security should be *the* goals for HRM. However, some firms' competitive strategies seem equally efficient if they emphasize extensive external recruitment, minimal training, early job responsibility, and an 'up or out' philosophy. Divisional companies could continually evaluate their HRM programmes, including assessment programmes, to determine which should be centralized and applied uniformly across business units and which should be decentralized to operating units. Business units may need to have HR programmes that will fit their business strategy at the same time as ensuring sufficient consistency to permit interdivisional transfer of talented managers.

Many of these attempted strategic shifts have profound impacts on the employees of an organization. Sonnenfeld *et al.* (1988) argue that their study of Harvard Business School MBAs seems to show that individuals graduate towards the kind of career system which best matches their personality. However, it may well be that organizational experiences themselves produce

changes in people; people do not have static, permanent person-
alities. Organizations which emphasize certain 'types' in their
socialization processes may in fact tend to *foster* certain changes
in people. In addition, though their research is a salutary remin-
der that selection is a two-way process, it is also likely that some
of the selecting was carried out by the organization, not by the
individual. People who fail to shine as a star should in a baseball
team may find that the organization is 'deselecting' them as much
as they are rejecting it.

Such strategic shifts place new demands on employees, dis-
rupting the psychological contract between organization and individual. Many people will have joined financial services
organizations in the 1970s and early 1980s because they seemed
to offer, in return for individual commitment and loyalty, job
security, stability and slow but steady promotion. However,
now such organizations are attempting to move towards more
entrepreneurial, risk-taking commercial cultures. Job security
may be threatened, old skills may be devalued and radical
changes in values demanded, such as a switch from respect-
ability, sobriety and a focus on thrift and saving to an emphasis
on flair, opportunism and lending. This shift may entail a massive
disruption of the psychological contract between employee and
employer, causing stress and discomfort, a loss of commitment
and a need for new human resource policies and systems to help
employees meet these new demands. Situations where one company, merging with another, seeks to radically redesign its culture may also create this kind of socio-psychological disruption or
rupture.

Assessment strategies and generic corporate strategies

There are other strategic frameworks in addition to Miles and
Snow (1984) which may be useful in developing assessment
options. For example, one can distinguish between three kinds
of corporate strategy pursued by companies – cost leadership,
differentiation, focus – drawing on the analysis of corporate strategy presented by Porter (1980). All have significant implications

for HRM practices in general, and assessment practices in particular. These strategies are often associated with different assessment choices, with reference to the following criteria:

Explicit job analysis	——	Implicit job analysis
Internal recruitment sources	——	External recruitment sources
Narrow career paths	——	Broad career paths
Single career paths	——	Multiple career ladders
Extensive work experience	——	Little work experience
Specialist background	——	Generalist experience
Explicit criteria	——	Results criteria
Closed assessment procedures	——	Open assessment procedure
Individual criteria	——	Group criteria
Short-term criteria	——	Long-term criteria
Low client participation	——	High client participation

Cost reduction/cost leadership strategies

The cost reducer strategy will try to produce goods and services more cheaply than competitors. It will emphasize efficiency of scale, minimization of expenses, high cost control, and the following of rules, regulations and plans. Power will tend to rest at the top, and competitor and consumer behaviour are usually seen as predictable. Such firms will try to increase productivity as they supply a standard, no frills, high volume product, with a constant pressure on production levels and employee numbers. They will often use part-time employees, sub-contractors, job simplification, automation and flexibility to reduce output cost per employee.

According to Schuler (1989) these organizations seem to require employees who display:

- repetitive and predictable behaviour
- a short-term focus
- individual activity
- a modest concern for quality
- a high concern for quantity and results
- low risk taking
- stability.

This implies the use of the following characteristics in assessment processes:

1 stable fixed job descriptions
2 recruitment for technical skills
3 narrow career paths
4 internal promotion
5 an emphasis on specialization, expertise and efficiency
6 a short-term, results-oriented approach
7 minimal training and development
8 close monitoring and control
9 individual criteria for appraisal.

Innovation strategies

Innovation strategies will depend on groups of highly trained specialists from various areas working together to design and produce rapidly changing products and services. They will require both differentiation and coordination, frequent face-to-face meetings, and decentralization of decision making. Authority will be based on expertise, with few standard procedures or bureaucratic rules, as the environment is perceived as dynamic, turbulent and uncertain.

These organizations seem to require:

1 creativity
2 a long-term focus
3 cooperation and interdependence
4 a moderate concern for quality and quantity
5 a concern for process and results
6 risk taking
7 tolerance of ambiguity.

This implies:

- implicit job analysis
- job flexibility
- long-term, group-based appraisals
- general skills

- broad career paths
- external recruitment
- process and results criteria in assessment
- extensive training and development.

Quality enhancement strategies

Quality enhancement strategies often attempt to deliver high quality goods and services, with total quality management targeted at suppliers and customers as well as the organization. Customers' desires and needs will drive the quality enhancement process, with an emphasis on unique specifications, customer orientation, and cooperation from all parts of the organization and industry chain. Distinctions between manufacturing and non-manufacturing organizations may become more blurred.

Assessment criteria here include:

1 relative predictability, stability
2 intermediate and long-term focus
3 moderate interdependence
4 a high concern for quality and process
5 a moderate concern for quantity
6 low risk taking
7 organizational commitment
8 flexibility and adaptability.

This implies the following assessment practices:

1 explicit job analysis
2 explicit job descriptions
3 employee autonomy and participation
4 individual and group criteria for appraisal
5 short-term appraisal
6 results-oriented appraisal
7 extensive training and development
8 some external recruitment
9 narrow career paths
10 internal promotion.

Box 2.2

Caledonian Paper at Irvine is the Scottish affiliate of the Finnish Kynmere Corp, a vertically integrated multinational active in the forest productions industry with 15 Finnish and three other European production sites. Its core business is the manufacture of paper especially fine paper, but it also makes wood-based panels and sawn timber and utilizes a large multinational network of agents and representatives.

As the largest printing paper producer in Europe and one of the most extensive lightweight coated mechanical paper (LWC) producer in the world, the fastest-growing segment of the market since 1985, it founded Caledonian Paper PLC (as a greenfield site) in 1987 as an integrated mill producing paper directly from raw wood in a continuous process and as the only UK-based supplier of LWC. A significant number of personnel, including the managing director, came from the Kaukus Oy mill in Finland.

Caledonian supplies the UK and selected European and other countries, in consultation with the parent country and with technical backup and R & D from Finland to develop a state of the art product. Marketing is, however, decentralized, with Caledonian responsible for its own market research and promotional activities. It seems as if Caledonian is operating with only limited autonomy, essentially as a 'miniature replica', with some likelihood of greater strategic independence in the future.

Caledonian has had some difficulty in recruiting people with specific skills, and has prized 'workforce flexibility' as a central component of its 'quality enhancement' strategy. This, it is argued, requires highly committed employees engaged in continuous training and development. A flat structure, team working, and multi-skilling are all used to reinforce flexibility, and it has made extensive use of psychometric tests to assess trainability, aptitude, motivation, and attitudes.

In many ways the selection process has followed the textbook strategic management model: human resource planning and assessment of structure and culture based on Finnish experience preceded interviews and testing by outside psychologists. It made extensive use of the 16PF personality inventory to assess flexibility and team orientation. Flexibility was seen as involving both a willingness to work in a multi-skilled way and willingness and ability to adjust to shift working. A job-positioning exercise to identify specific jobs was held and training, including for many training in Finland, followed selection. As a greenfield site the recruitment, assessment and selection lever is an option less available elsewhere.

(*Source:* Beaumont, 1993)

One Scottish affiliate of a Finnish multinational has sought to use assessment processes, especially psychometric assessment, to pursue a quality enhancement strategy, as Box 2.2 shows.

Conclusions

In this chapter we have considered the management of assessment from the point of view of strategic management, exploring relationships between corporate strategy, structure and life-cycle stage and the nature of assessment systems and processes. Most research in this area has been prescriptive, following Tichy *et al.*'s (1982) model of strategic HRM which argued that 'different strategies have different implications for the nature, role and importance of human resource management (HRM) and selection' (Williams and Dobson, 1995: 1). As the authors themselves note, the major concern in this perspective is with strategic selection and the role that selection can play in promoting strategic change; but most theorizing over-emphasizes the rational in organizational decision making and under-emphasizes the emergent, the satisfying and the political in strategic management (e.g. Mintzberg, 1988). As a result of its rational, objective, managerialist, unitary and conflict-free view of organizational life, the strategic management model of assessment shares many epistemological and methodological assumptions with the psychometric model, and both share a common heritage in US behavioural science. Indeed, the strategic management model is often content to pose 'who', 'why' and 'when' questions to assessment processes, leaving the 'how' questions of method and technique to psychometrics.

Most research has been guided by the 'matching' or 'contingent' tradition of strategic HRM, taking business strategy as a first-order, primary process and seeking to 'match' or 'integrate' HRM policies and practices with it as second-order processes. As Williams and Dobson (1995: 1) put it, 'our primary purpose . . . is to introduce conceptual frameworks that will change with the role and design of selection systems . . . so as to achieve their strategic objectives more effectively'. A variety of such frameworks have been considered in this chapter. First, we explored the relationship between corporate strategy and human resource planning systems, before exploring links between organizational structure and assessment processes. Secondly, we considered in detail the nature of organizational strategy, its relationship with assessment, and the implications of strategic choice and strategic change for managing assessment. A number of authors (e.g. Purcell, 1989) have distinguished between corporate, business level and functional strategies, seeing HRM strategies as functional level strategies concerned with the attainment of business goals. HRM is thus primarily reactive, making little contribution to strategic choice. In many conceptualizations, the focus of assessment is the identification and measurement of behavioural role requirements following strategic selection, often using some version of Porter's generic strategies, e.g. Schuler and Jackson's (1987) translation of strategy into role requirements, Caledonian Papers' attempt to translate a quality enhancement strategy into assessment requirements and National and Provincial's attempt to derive structural and role requirements and behavioural expectations from choice of mission and cultures (Boxes 2.1 and 2.2). In Chapter 6 we shall consider one perspective on facilitating this matching or translation process, the competency approach. Here we will simply note that there are other versions of such matching processes (e.g. Miles and Snow's (1984) strategic types, Sonnenfeld and Peiperl's (1988) translation of them into career systems) and that all run the danger of moving from loose analytical framework to tight prescriptive commandments. Similar concerns apply to life-cycle and portfolio planning models, often based on some version of the Boston Consulting Group model. Just as businesses can be classified into stars, question marks, cash cows and dogs according to market share and market growth rate, so can people in terms of performance and potential (with some relabelling, the general idea is to regularly shine the stars with rewards, milk the steady, reliable cash-cows, shoot the lazy dogs and feed the horses!). Others have extended this to exploring the different strategic implications of businesses at different stages of development (e.g. Kochan and Barocci, 1985; Baird and Meshoulam, 1988). Start-up, question-mark businesses will seek to head-hunt the best available talent externally; growth or star businesses will place more emphasis on formal assessment, internal labour markets and succession planning and career development; mature or cash cow businesses will have well-developed, formalized assessment systems emphasizing internal mobility; and declining or dog businesses will have reduced investment in HRM and a growing emphasis on downsizing, workforce reduction and redeployment.

An increasing interest in this area has been shown in 'selecting for innovation' as part of an 'innovation' strategy, exploring the personal characteristics of innovative and creative people (e.g. Kirton's (1976) 'Adaptation–Innovation Inventory' and attempts to assess by personality inventories such qualities as desire for autonomy, independence, tolerance for ambiguity and a propensity for risk taking, e.g. Williams and Dobson, 1995). Often this strategic requirement is immediately operationalized into a personality trait to be assessed psychometrically, an example of the often close relationship between the strategic management and psychometric models (with little empirical evidence for their effectiveness). More sophisticated models (e.g. King and Anderson, 1995) also take into account workgroup and team climate factors, and the role of work and organizational factors in innovative production.

As we have noted, 'matching' models of the relationships between strategy and selection have been criticized for their reactive nature, their managerialism, their neglect of other stakeholders, their unitary view of organizations, their neglect of political and conflict processes, and their over-rational, positivistic knowledge base, both in terms of the model of strategy offered and in terms of their conception of the assessment process (supplied by the psychometric model). A more recent emergent model in strategic management is the resource-based view of the firm (e.g. Grant,

1991; Kamoche, 1994; Wright *et al.*, 1994). Since this framework lays greater stress on the firm's internal resources and capabilities, in particular its human resources as embodied in employee skills, knowledge, and other attributes, then it promises to place the management of assessment in a more central, proactive place than that suggested by the 'matching' models. We shall explore this strategic management perspective in more depth in Chapter 5 when we discuss the 'core competence' approach to strategy (e.g. Hamel and Prahalad, 1994). However, though some argue that HRM practices in general are too well known and imitable to provide a source of sustained competitive advantage (Wright *et al.*, 1994), it may be that the tacit knowledge, organizational capabilities and processual skills involved in developing firm-specific assessment strategies may help organizations able to develop scarce, innovative, inimitable, durable and non-substitutable assessment strategies gain strategic value. This is also an issue explored in Chapter 6.

In this chapter we have emphasized the strategic role that assessment and selection processes can play, illustrated by means of several case studies of leading companies. Some useful frameworks for thinking about this strategic role of assessment have been introduced, such as considering the relationship between assessment processes and corporate strategy, organizational structure, business/product life cycle and job design. In the course of this discussion, several methods of assessment and selection have been mentioned. In the next chapter, assessment methods are more fully discussed, reviewed and evaluated. This focus on the technology of assessment is the major contribution of the psychometric perspective on assessment.

3

THE PSYCHOMETRIC PERSPECTIVE

A major concern of the psychometric perspective on assessment and selection, as described in the introduction, is the technology and efficiency of selection, and in particular the development of methods of assessment and of models of validating their effectiveness.

A wide range of selection and assessment methods now exist, and others are emerging all the time. They can be classified in various ways. One is to classify them according to what it is they are trying to assess – whether it is abilities, aptitudes, personality traits, motives, interests, preferences or styles, skills or behaviour. Another approach, taken by Robertson and Iles (1988) is to classify them in terms of whether they are past, present, or future oriented. *Past*-oriented methods attempt to assess past behaviours, on the grounds that these are the best predictors of future behaviour. Such methods include the traditional application form asking for educational history and track record; the curriculum vitae or résumé; the taking up of references; and more systematic methods to score life history data and biographical information (biodata) or career and life accomplishments (e.g. the accomplishment record or career portfolio). Some kinds of structured interview techniques such as the patterned behaviour description interview, or some kinds of criterion-referenced interview also explore past behaviour as a guide to future conduct. Rather than ask candidates about how they would deal with conflict or handle a presentation, for example, these ask for examples of how the candidate had previously handled conflict at work or made a presentation. Peer assessment or supervisor assessment methods used to make promotion decisions also explore past behaviour.

Other methods attempt to examine *present* behaviour and skills. These include those kinds of often poorly conducted interviews which attempt to assess a candidate's personality, oral communication skills or motivation levels; cognitive ability tests which attempt to assess present levels of mental functioning; personality and interest inventories which attempt to assess other aspects of individual differences; and inventories which attempt to assess not so much levels of functioning as *styles* of functioning – candidate preferences for innovating, taking up particular team roles, taking in information, making decisions, or learning, for example. Other present-oriented methods include the range of work sample and situational tests which give candidates a sample or facsimile of the job in question, and assess the candidate's ability to perform. Typing tests and flight simulators are two examples; another is the assessment centre, where typically managerial or professional candidates are given scenarios such as an in-basket exercise, a presentation, a group meeting, a role play and an interview. Their performance in these activities is then assessed against the specific job-related criteria (e.g. communication skills, administrative skills, leadership skills, ability to manage conflict) judged necessary for effective performance through a job analysis.

Some methods attempt to assess *future* intentions and performance. Many unstructured and poorly conducted interviews often pose rhetorical or hypothetical questions to candidates of the 'what would you do if' kind. The answers candidates give are rarely indicative of how they actually *would* perform in such situations. However, some more rigorous and systematic kinds of future-oriented methods and scales have been developed. One is the *situational interview*. Here candidates are presented with scenarios judged to be critically important to successful job performance (e.g. responding to a difficult customer or employee).

Their answers as to how they would respond are scored against a predetermined scale of answers ranging from poor answers (e.g. ignore it) to very good answers (e.g. take action of an appropriate kind). Such interviews have been shown to be moderately predictive of job performance for supervisory posts in the USA (e.g. Latham *et al.*, 1980) and managerial jobs in the UK (e.g. Robertson *et al.*, 1991). Another kind of future-oriented scale is the *managerial self-efficacy* scale. This presents candidates with a list of required managerial tasks, as determined by a job analysis, and asks them to state how confident they are that they could perform them. Self-efficacy, the degree to which a person feels confident about performing a required task, has been shown to be very important in a range of clinical settings involving phobias and the like, and it has also been shown to be moderately predictive of managerial performance (Robertson and Sadri, 1993). Clearly there are other kinds of self-assessment techniques, and self-assessment is a method of growing importance, particularly in promoting self-development. Its role in selection has been more open to question, however, as it is believed that candidates wanting a job will be self-serving and lenient on themselves. It appears to be an area subject to cultural factors, as Americans appear to over-state their self-assessed abilities, Asians to under-state them (Muchinsky, 1994).

There are many other techniques more difficult to classify, such as astrology and graphology (handwriting analysis), both of doubtful validity as predictors of job success (though often used in continental Europe, especially France). Other methods are beginning to be employed more often, especially in the USA. These include drug testing, integrity testing and medical and physical examinations, as well as genetic screening.

Evaluating assessment methods from a psychometric perspective

Whatever method is used, the major 'evaluative standards' or criteria by which a method has been assessed has been the traditional psychometric ones of reliability (is it measuring something accurately?) and validity (is it measuring what it purports to measure?). In terms of validity, the major dimension of importance has been criterion-related or predictive validity. That is, does the assessment method actually predict job performance? (or some related criterion, such as tenure, absenteeism, training success or career level). This relationship between predictor (the method) and criterion (the index of performance) is usually expressed in terms of a *validity coefficient*, or correlation between predictor score and criterion score.

By *reliability* is meant the extent to which scores on a measure are free from random error – a concept similar to that of 'consistency'. This is important; but what we also want to know is whether what is being measured is in fact what our measuring instrument claims it is measuring: that is, the *validity* of the measuring instrument.

For human resource practitioners as distinct from psychologists, the most important consideration is perhaps *criterion-related validity* – to what extent do candidates' scores on a test, exercise or interview predict future job success, as measured by criteria such as output or rated performance?

Coming out well in terms of predictive validity are assessment centres, work samples and peer evaluation. Ability tests and biodata also perform well, while references, interviews and personality tests perform relatively badly. However, later research has shown that interviews, especially structured, job-related interviews such as situational interviews based on a thorough job analysis and targeted on specific competencies, are much better predictors of job performance than has been traditionally thought, and are certainly as good as biodata (Smith and Robertson, 1989). Studies of more up-to-date, work-centred personality tests (such as the Occupational Personality Questionnaire) have also shown them to be much better predictors than traditional clinical or projective tests and at least as good as, if not better than, biodata. Note that, despite its extensive use in France, Israel and elsewhere, there is little systematic evidence for the validity of graphology or handwriting analysis (see, for example, Smith and Robertson, 1989).

Predictive or criterion-related validity is clearly an important consideration. It is not the only relevant standard, however. Another standard against which assessment procedures can be evaluated is their potential for *bias* against specific groups, as women, people with disabilities, racial and ethnic minorities older people. One way of looking at this is through the adverse impact of a procedure, that is, the degree to which it rejects a disproportionate number of applicants from that group, or screens out group members unfairly.

There are some methods which perform poorly on both criteria, such as references or unstructured interviews. Other techniques perform moderately well on both criteria, such as biodata, personality inventories and structured interviews. Tests of cognitive ability seem to display relatively high validity alongside relatively high potential for bias. Some methods, such as work sample tests and assessment centres, seem to perform well on both criteria. These two latter methods seem to display high predictive validity and also appear to be generally fair to minority groups and women; in all cases continual monitoring is needed to check for bias.

However, there are other evaluative standards which could be used. One is the *utility* of the measure, or the monetary *value* of selection and the monetary benefits a selection procedure might confer. It appears that work samples and assessment centres come out very well on this criterion, despite the apparently high initial costs of setting them up. What is regarded as beyond doubt is the considerable financial benefit, in terms of improved productivity, of using valid selection techniques (e.g. Williams and Dobson, 1995).

Many commonly used methods (e.g. unstructured interviews, references) do not come out very well as predictors of job success, not much better than astrology or guesswork. However, some other methods – work samples, assessment centres, structured interviews, cognitive ability tests, work-oriented personality inventories – appear to perform much better.

The overall message after several decades of research is that, taking into account all the problems and limitations, some methods – such as psychometric tests of ability, more modern tests of personality, work samples, assessment centres and structured, job-related interviews – are relatively valid predictors of job performance, while references, graphology and unstructured interviews are not and should not be used for selection purposes.

such

g is that, by and large, many organizations
this message, despite the extremely impress-
ts that valid techniques confer in terms of
nd productivity, shorter training times, lower
er person–job fit.

ll look at some of the reasons as to why organizations ᵕ inue to use methods of doubtful validity and do
not use the better-regarded methods. In doing so we will argue
that reliability and validity – whether criterion-related predictive
validity or what is known as construct validity and content validity – are not the only criteria or standards organizations use to
assess assessment methods. Other standards – including its fairness or bias, its utility or financial benefit conferred on the organization using it, its acceptability and applicability, and its impact
on candidates – also need to be considered. This finding has
stimulated research into selection and assessment from a social
process perspective, considered in Chapter 4. First, we will
review some common assessment methods as seen from a
psychometric perspective.

A detailed look at some selection and assessment methods

For the purpose of this analysis, we will classify assessment
methods into five categories:

1 interviews
2 tests
3 inventories
4 simulations
5 other methods.

Let us start with the interview, which remains almost ubiqui-
tous.

The interview

There are many different types of interview. Some interviews are
conducted on a one-to-one basis, others (especially in the UK

public sector) by a panel of interviewers. Some interviews are essentially *unstructured*, resembling informal conversations. In this case the interviewer is free to ask whatever questions in whatever order he or she likes, often attempting to assess (usually unsuccessfully) the personality, motivation or skills of the candidate. Other interviews are more structured or standardized – the criteria the interview is designed to assess are derived in advance through a job analysis and spelt out in a person specification; the kind of questions put to candidates (and even the order in which they are put) may, in extremely structured interviews, follow a predetermined pattern. This strategy may sometimes be undertaken to minimize the chances of bias and unfair discrimination against minorities and women; sometimes to maximize validity. One kind of structured interview is the *criterion-referenced* interview, which explores how candidates handled in the past incidents which exemplify the need to demonstrate the relevant criteria (communication, teamwork or conflict management skills, for example). A similar, more rigorous example is the *patterned behaviour description interview* which focuses on job requirements and on critical incidents of past performance. Another more future-oriented interview is the *situational interview*, where candidates are presented with scenarios representing critical incidents to be faced on the job and have their answers scored against predetermined benchmarks indicating poor, average or good responses.

Interviews in general are useful to gain background information on individuals; in particular how they see their past, present and future. Unlike other, more narrow and specific instruments, they can be used to assess a wide range of qualities, such as knowledge, skills and abilities. They are often perceived by the candidate as face valid, and are useful in establishing rapport with a candidate. They can also be used to get a feeling for the candidate's motivation, to clarify issues and to obtain apparently 'live' examples of interpersonal skills. They are useful for developing hypotheses which can be followed up later and are also useful in recruiting the candidate, presenting the organization in a positive light and stressing its advantages.

However, the interview has long been perceived from a psychometric perspective as of doubtful usefulness as a selection instrument, because interviewers are prone to make a series of errors. These include:

- first impression effects: basing judgements on the immediate impression made by the candidate, usually non-verbally in terms of age, gender, appearance, race, eye contact, smiles and other gestures
- compatibility effects: demographic or other similarities to the candidate bias other judgements (e.g. religion, gender, race, school attended)
- halo and horns effects: judgements on other dimensions are biased negatively or positively by judgements on one key dimension (e.g. dislike may generate lower ratings generally, liking the candidate may give higher ratings)
- leniency errors, such as tending to score all candidates highly
- central tendency errors, such as tending to give all candidates average scores
- contrast effects, such as comparing candidates with each other rather than against criteria.

A review of the validity of the employment interview (Marchese and Muchinsky, 1993) showed that interview *structure* appeared to be the only characteristic moderating interview validity. Unlike earlier views of interview invalidity, their estimated true validity (0.38) indicates that the interview can have moderately high validity as a selection device, especially if structured interviews are used. Superior predictive validity is associated with structured interviews. A US study of the past-oriented patterned behaviour description interview showed that it was rated as slightly more difficult and stressful than a conventional unstructured interview, but that both interviewers and candidates (especially interviewers) found it more complete, more thorough, fairer and as yielding a more complete picture of job requirements (Janz and Mooney, 1993).

Tests

There are many kinds of tests, ranging from timed to untimed tests and from fixed answer to open response tests. Perhaps the most important distinction here is between 'cognitive ability' tests and tests of job knowledge or expertise. The distinguishing feature of a *test* (as distinct from an inventory or a questionnaire) is that it provides a standardized score where 'more' does mean 'better' (unlike the situation with personality trait measures), and where external factors are sufficiently controlled to make individual results comparable. These factors point to the advantages of tests: they provide accurate quantitative measures, rendering comparison between individuals possible, and they are by and large relatively easy to administer and score. Tests also in general appear both reliable and valid, predicting job performance at all levels, but especially in more complex jobs. However, tests show disadvantages. They are not necessarily popular with candidates, who may not perceive their relationship to job performance. Some tests depend on language skills, which render them susceptible to bias against minority groups in particular.

In addition to psychometric tests of mental ability (e.g. of cognitive abilities, such as verbal, numerical or spatial abilities, creativity, or critical thinking), 'job knowledge' tests have also been developed. One review showed that such written tests were good predictors of both job performance and training success, and that such tests were more valid for more complex jobs (Dye *et al.*, 1993).

Inventories

Various kinds of inventories, as distinct from tests, exist. Some attempt to measure personality or personal attributes – traits that appear to underlie behaviour (e.g. sociability, assertiveness, dominance). Others assess interests, values or general motivational factors, and are useful in career counselling or development rather than selection. Inventories can also provide quantifiable scores, allowing comparison between individuals. Norms for specific groups (managers, accountants, etc.) can also be generated to show how individuals compare in terms of their profiles compared to that group's profile.

However, some participants can give 'socially desirable' responses, and others may find certain items offensive or of doubtful relevance to job performance. More work-oriented inventories, such as Saville and Holdsworth's Occupational

---

Box 3.1

The CSQ is based on a job analysis of customer service jobs to identify those dimensions related to successful performance, and has both British and Chinese norms. It consists of eleven dimensions grouped under three headings. Need to control, sociability, group orientation, attitude to authority comprise 'relations with people'; understanding of people, mental awareness, attitude to change, and approach to organizing constitute 'thinking style'; emotional sensitivity, need for results and need for social approval constitute 'emotions and energy'.

In a validation study, only one factor (respect for authority) correlated with certified absence, whereas three factors correlated with punctuality and uncertified absence. More interestingly, four factors (sociability, attitude to change, sensitivity, and need for results) correlated with number of compliments received, while four others correlated with number of errors noted. Only attitude to change correlated with an overall score, comprised of absenteeism, punctuality, compliments, errors, and appraisal data. The researcher concluded that 'it may be time to revise the CSQ . . . to include fewer factors but ones which are demonstrably related to customer service per se'.

(Furnham, 1994)

Personality Questionnaire (OPQ) may be less susceptible in this respect. If based on a job analysis, some work-oriented personality inventories have been shown to be of moderate validity in predicting job performance.

We have already seen (Box 2.2) how one Finnish multinational has used personality inventories such as the 16PF to assess for flexibility as part of its overall quality enhancement strategy. A Hong Kong-based multinational, the airline Cathay Pacific, uses another personality inventory, Saville and Holdsworth's Customer Service Questionnaire (CSQ) to assess its staff in terms of how strongly they are oriented to deliver customer service, which Cathay Pacific sees as a key source of competitive advantage (Box 3.1).

Another recent development in personality inventories, especially in the USA, has been to devise 'integrity' or 'honesty' tests to assess conscientiousness, reliability or responsibility. Many are untested but one Canadian study (Woolley and Hakstian, 1993) showed that such tests could predict 'counter-productivity' or self-reported deviance. However, this was also true of mainstream personality tests. Murphy and Lee (1994) pointed out that while integrity test scores do seem related to measures of overall job performance, both integrity and performance measures may be related to the personality trait 'conscientiousness'. However, there appear to be logical and empirical distinctions between conscientiousness and the more complex, less understood construct of 'integrity'. It is the currently held view of personality psychometricians that there are five established, well-understood personality dimensions – the so-called 'Big Five' (Robertson and Hesketh, 1993). These are variously labelled neuroticism, extraversion, agreeableness, conscientiousness, and openness to experience. The two dimensions with the most predictive potential for selection purposes seem to be conscientiousness (correlated with motivation, performance, dependability, carefulness and responsibility) and openness to experience (correlated with capacity to learn, training proficiency and ability).

Simulations

Simulations attempt to 'sample' aspects of the job, so that facsimiles of the job are presented to candidates. They range from simple typing tests to complex flight simulators. In managerial settings simulations typically include in-basket exercises, presentations, group meetings and one-to-one role plays or interviews, and these are typically combined into an *assessment centre*. The strengths of simulations are that they can be used to collect evidence of actual behaviours, rather than intentions or claims, and can be used to assess skills and weaknesses and potential for higher-level positions. They can also often appear realistic and face valid to candidates and can give candidates a taste or 'realistic preview' of the job in question, allowing them to 'select out' if it does not appear to meet their needs or match their abilities. The use of common standardized stimuli and exercises permits consistent standards to be applied across candidate performance.

However, simulations require well-trained observers and can

Box 3.2

A north east USA-based bank losing market share to competitors following deregulation sought to change its culture towards a more differentiated, sales-oriented culture. While one group of employees would remain in routine service roles, another would be more sale oriented. The bank needed to identify managers, sales representatives and service personnel from the existing pool, and to foster cooperation between sales and service teams. A six-step career path was established for service personnel, while new sales jobs were created.

Employees were given the opportunity to nominate themselves for sales or service jobs, and criteria were developed for the various jobs available. One assessment tool consisted of a set of written and oral work samples describing typical situations. Using model responses and scoring sheet, the samples were designed to evaluate performance in real work situations, expose candidates to aspects of the new jobs, and provide evidence of oral communication and thinking skills. Alongside appraisal and interview data, information from the samples was used to select and place candidates.

(Hobson and Lipsett, 1993)

---

be expensive and time consuming to set up and run. They do appear, however, to show high predictive validity and little bias, and are generally highly regarded by participants (see Box 3.2).

Work sample tests have been extensively used in the UK by large public organizations wishing to introduce objective, rational, transparent, fair and job-based recruitment systems for train drivers, fire fighters, clerks and managers (Wood, 1994). Such samples or facsimiles are constructed through analysing specific job behaviours, selecting a sample of tasks, translating the samples into test items, developing standardized administration procedures and implementing scoring procedures. Some form of 'back translation' should be carried out by independent observers to ascertain that the job can be 'recovered' from its items. For example, Dorset Training and Enterprise Council has developed work sample tests which training providers may use. Individuals can be given opportunities to experience typical bricklaying activities such as using a trowel and mortar, building a short length of wall, marking out a shape, and reproducing a wire form. This is intended to enable them and the provider to determine their suitability for a bricklaying career.

In addition to being at least as valid as psychometric tests, work samples have the advantage of being more positively regarded by candidates and appear to be less biased against minority groups. They can be used in the form of 'trainability tests' which offer training before testing to equalize prior levels of skill. The ability to learn parts of the job and the rate at which this is done are regarded as predictive of job success (Robertson and Kandola, 1982).

In a managerial context, the major work samples employed are the in-basket or in-tray exercise and the group discussion, often included in an assessment centre.

Assessment centres

Assessment centres are used extensively for military and police officers, fire fighters and administrators. Candidates are all assessed against a set of predetermined criteria held to be essential for job success through prior job analysis as they attempt a series of activities or exercises. These may include psychometric tests or work samples. Commonly used samples include various decision-making exercises, presentations, role plays and 'in-basket' or 'in-tray' exercises to assess administrative abilities. Here candidates typically review their actions with assessors, who then assess performance against relevant dimensions. For example, one Canadian telephone company uses the Telephone Supervisor In Basket Exercise, where candidates assume the role of new first level manager and deal with scheduling, productivity, PR and personal problems presented in their 'in-tray' (Hakstian and Harlos, 1993).

Assessment centres have been repeatedly shown by empirical research to be the most valid predictor of managerial potential (Gaugler et al., 1987), to be generally fair to minorities and women, and to be well regarded by participants, both those accepted by the centre process and those rejected. For example, Iles (1991) showed that overall assessment ratings in a Cooperative

Bank centre were not related to gender or appearance, while Robertson and Iles (1988) showed that participants in a National Westminster Bank Centre regarded it more positively in terms of fairness, accuracy and development value than other techniques, such as biodata or situational interviews (Robertson *et al.*, 1991).

Assessment centres are widely used not only in the USA and UK but also in the Netherlands. For example the Dutch company KPN, formed from the privatization of the state Netherlands Postal and Telecommunications Services in 1989, used a stage model for graduate selection, employing successively application forms, a recruitment interview, a mental test, a management interview, and a final assessment centre. The centre consists of a group discussion attempting to resolve a business problem, and mixed both competition and collaboration. A case interview with two assessors around a business case where the candidate has to propose an analysis and a plan of action was also used. Overall, the candidates were assessed against six dimensions: thinking power, verbal ability, interpersonal effectiveness, firmness, ambition and operational power. The recruitment and management interviews were designed to assess all six dimensions; the assessment centre was designed to assess only thinking power, interpersonal effectiveness, and firmness (defined here as independence, strength, resistance, decisiveness, stamina, ability to cope with stress). A validation study showed that the overall assessment centre rating was a good predictor of present salary, whereas verbal ability as measured in the mental test was *negatively* correlated with salary progression. Firmness as assessed by the recruitment officer also bore no relation to salary progression, whereas it did when assessed in the assessment centre (Jansen and Stoop, 1994).

Assessment centres are also used extensively in the UK public sector to assess potential, select for training programmes, and identify development needs. Some national health authorities in the 1980s began using assessment centres to identify candidates for the General Management Training Scheme Stage 3. One kind of centre used by two health authorities used repertory grid and critical incident techniques to analyse the jobs of general managers. It identified 10 criteria or performance dimensions as critical to performance in this role:

1 leadership
2 communication
3 influence
4 people orientation
5 strategic planning
6 innovation
7 analytical reasoning
8 decision making
9 achievement orientation
10 resilience.

Candidates were assessed against these criteria in a two-day assessment centre consisting of:

- an assigned role group exercise on resource allocation
- an 'unassigned' group exercise on proposals for a performance review
- an in-tray exercise
- a verbal and numerical critical reasoning test
- a productive thinking test
- a personality questionnaire
- an oral presentation
- a career development interview.

However, in recent years there have been extensive moves away from using centres to assess and select staff towards using them to identify training needs; in this context they are often termed 'development centres'.

For example, City University has used development centres (termed 'management development workshops') making exhaustive use of self and peer assessment. The aims were to develop awareness of managerial strengths and weaknesses, develop skills in assessment and feedback, and encourage development plans. Using a competency model to denote behavioural requirements (problem solving, task managing, managing people, and managing oneself) and employing several activities (leaderless group exercise, in-basket, presentation, and a competencies profile questionnaire), it also used video playback after each exercise to focus self-assessment. Discussions with a partner and the group as a whole generated a final assessment (Williams and Dobson, 1995).

Evaluation of the psychometric perspective

The central contention of the psychometric perspective is that psychological differences between people are measurable, and are important in determining job performance. The major research goal has been to identify links between individual differences (conceived mainly in terms of ability, aptitude, skill, personality, style and, as we shall see in Chapter 6 competencies) and job performance. This involves the measurement of job success (criteria), the assessment of individual differences (predictors) and the measurement of the relationship between the two (expressed as a correlation coefficient or coefficient of validity). Major criteria of success include performance, as assessed by productivity or supervisor ratings; absenteeism; tenure; and progression and training performance. Many predictors show different relationships to these criteria, and not all criteria can either be measured accurately or regarded as appropriate indicators of job success. In addition, other factors than individual differences clearly affect job performance (e.g. supervisory style, job design, organizational culture, etc.), limiting the effectiveness of selection decisions.

Job analysis is usually recommended as a first stage in designing a selection system, followed by the identification of attributes required by successful candidates. In classical psychometric theory, these are seen as rather general, abstract 'signs' such as cognitive ability (usually seen as hierarchical, incorporating a general mental ability as a factor and subfactors such as spatial, verbal and numerical ability) and personality, now generally conceived of as involving the Big 5 major factors of extroversion, neuroticism, openness to experience, conscientiousness and agreeableness. However, more recently skills and competencies, seen by psychometricians as less fundamental constructs, have come to play a major role in selection research; an area explored in more depth in Chapter 6.

One limitation of the model is that job analysis and the identification of job success factors assumes a stable set of job demands, yet often the job for which prediction is to be made is newly created, may change over time, or may be subject to negotiation and change. In addition, there are difficulties in translating job characteristics into personal attributes or success factors. Researchers in this tradition probably see three relatively recent developments (meta-analysis, validity generalization and utility theory) as the 'crown jewels' of contemporary psychometric selection theory. Hunter and Schmidt (1990) focused on sampling error and other 'artifactual' features of local validation studies and developed statistical procedures for combining such results, while removing effects of range restriction (where the span of scores on criteria and predictor measures does not cover the full range available) and measurement unreliability. Such factors may give misleading impressions of the underlying relationship between predictor and criteria, and hence misleadingly low impressions of predictive validity. Such meta-analyses when conducted have tended to show that the major selection methods such as tests, work samples and assessment centres are more valid than was thought before the 1980s. In addition, the development of utility procedures to establish the financial gain available from selection methods has also been regarded as a significant recent development. Taking selection ratios (the ratios of jobs to candidates) into account, the financial gains from better selection are then calculable, and appear to be substantial, especially in situations where the financial gain from improved job performance is considerable (e.g. Boudreau, 1989). Such developments put some flesh on the claims of the resource-based view of the firm (considered in Chapter 2) that human resources and human resource practices can confer significant sources of competitive advantage to organizations (e.g. Wright et al., 1994).

However, as we noted in Chapter 1, there have been a number of major challenges to this tradition. A strongly argued recent critique comes from Herriot and Anderson (1997), who claim that the tradition is in danger of terminal decline, facing unparalleled threats and becoming noticeably archaic and obsolete. The authors aim their critique primarily from a perspective informed by strategic management theory, outlined in Chapter 2. They see the traditional psychometric model as rooted in an era of bureaucracy and large numbers of stable, specialized jobs.

Post-bureaucratic forms of organization, changes in the global business environment, the growth of newly created roles, team-working and flexible work roles, the need to assess organizational rather than job fit, and the rise of deselection have all put pressure on it, rendering it out-moded and in danger of decline and marginalization. Environmental drivers like globalization, information technology, knowledge-based workers, learning organizations and the pace of change generally have all put pressure on traditional work-roles, as have movements to restructuring, requirements for flexibility and innovation, team working and modification to psychological (as well as employment) contracts. The dominant 'predictivist' model is thus seen as an impediment to responding adequately to such changes.

The dominant paradigm assumes that selection is of individuals (rather than teams), for stable long-term jobs (rather than flexible, newly created roles) in stable bureaucracies (rather than new forms of organization), and searches for person–job fit (rather than person–team or person–organization fit). It is argued that the dominant paradigm assumes that personnel psychology is a science, is universal, and is best advanced by objective analysis, methodological rigour, and quantitative methods; a culture that militates against innovation, adaptability and relevance by encouraging epistemological conformity, a lack of questioning of paradigm assumptions, and a commitment to a conservative and restrictive positivism, managerialism and empiricism.

There is, therefore, a need to open up this area, introduce other perspectives drawn from strategic management (itself dominated by unitarist and managerialist perspectives, as we saw in Chapter 2), social psychology, sociology and critical theory. Characterizing the dominant paradigm as a 'psychic prison', Herriot and Anderson (1997) argue for a focus on selection processes rather than methods, on developmental processes, on the impact of selection procedures, on applicant rights, on candidate decision making, on impression management by recruiters and candidates, on the development of the psychological contract and the socialization impact of selection methods, on changes in the job role which alter the criterion domain, on selection for organizational and team fit, on why discrimination occurs, and on cultural, national, historical and societal impacts on assessment processes. All these are issues which are beginning to be addressed by the 'social process' perspective discussed in Chapter 4.

In particular, Herriot and Anderson (1997) launch an attack on the crown jewels of the psychometric paradigm: utility analysis and meta-analysis. Many papers in this area have assumed that financial pay back is or will be a major factor in the selection of assessment methods by practitioners, yet experienced managers appear *less* likely to implement valid selection methods when given such calculations! (Latham and Whyte, 1994). Herriot and Anderson (1996) themselves argue that four main issues need to be addressed: selection for change, including selection for emergent predictors such as flexibility and innovation potential; the need for ongoing, internal reassessment rather than assessment solely on organizational entry; multiple and interactive levels of analysis, such as person–team and person–organization fit; and the generation of wider theoretical perspectives and innovative frameworks. Here they refer, for example, to selection as the domination of one group over another (e.g. Hollway, 1991), and to the need to ask why and for what purpose questions more frequently. However, their analysis remains undeveloped in this area, and is taken up more fully in Chapter 5. The major area that Herriot and Anderson (1997) identify as needing to be addressed in a modified selection paradigm is the need to adopt a multicultural framework, since the present dominant model reflects a largely Anglo-American world view which prizes universalism, individualism, reliability, specificity, achievement and an internal locus of control. Diversity in selection practice is one of the major concerns of the social process perspective on selection and assessment, to which we now turn.

4

A SOCIAL PROCESS
PERSPECTIVE

The social process model of assessment, as we have seen in Chapter 1, is primarily derived from European social psychology and interactionist sociology, rather than US differential psychology. Its concerns are rather different, as its interest is less in the prediction of job performance than in understanding the relationships between applicant, recruiter, assessment instrument, organization and the micro and macro social context in which assessment is conducted. As a result, major theoretical tools are constructs of identity, negotiation, interaction, attitude, attribution, impact, culture and climate, and its favoured research instruments are not the job analysis questionnaire, the psychometric test and the supervisor rating of performance but observations of and interviews with applicants and recruiters in assessment situations, whether in the laboratory (the favoured US technique) or in the field (the favoured European technique). Perhaps because it is often self-consciously European in its stance *vis-à-vis* North America, it has a greater sensitivity to issues of culture and diversity. This is partly shown in its readiness to explore assessment practices in different cultural and social contexts, rather than assume that the abstract generalizations of Anglo-American psychometric psychology in relation to utility, validity generalization and meta-analysis apply universally and unquestioningly.

Analysis of selection and assessment practice in different (mainly Western industrial) countries reveals an interesting pattern of similarities and differences. The social process perspective is particularly interested in such patterns, as well as in issues of negotiation, self-concept and impact.

Different national practices

The United Kingdom

There have been three large-scale surveys of the methods used by large UK companies to select staff. Two surveys concentrated on managerial selection. One on the top 1000 UK companies published by Robertson and Makin (1986) showed that interviews and references remained by far the most popular techniques. Psychological testing was used by 36 per cent, graphology by 8 per cent and biodata by 6 per cent of companies. A more recent study by Shackleton and Newell (1991) reported somewhat greater use of both interviews and references, substantially greater use of psychological testing (65 per cent) and biodata (10 per cent), and less use of graphology (3 per cent). A survey of employee selection methods used across staff categories by the Institute of Manpower Studies (Bevan and Fryatt, 1988) confirmed the widespread use of interviews (91 per cent) and references (85 per cent) but reported less widespread use of psychological testing (21 per cent). Psychometric tests, whether of personality or cognitive ability, seem to be used more often for managerial selection than for most other categories of staff.

Interestingly, recruitment consultancies, whether search or selection consultancies, seem to show substantially the same pattern of use. A study of 50 UK consultancies by Clarke (1993) reported that interviews were almost ubiquitously used, with references used by over 80 per cent of respondents. Psychological testing was employed by over 40 per cent of respondents and biodata by over 11 per cent, though graphology was only marginally used (3 per cent, mainly by continental, European owned or associated firms).

With regard to assessment centres, it appears that over one

quarter of large UK companies may now use them, compared to only around 10 per cent of companies in the 1970s (Mabey and Iles, 1991; Shackleton and Newell, 1991).

Flanders (Belgium)

A study by De Witte *et al.* (1992) of selection practices in Flanders (Flemish speaking Belgium) shows a similar pattern to the UK situation. The most commonly used technique was the interview, followed by intelligence tests and personality inventories (63 per cent each). References were somewhat less commonly used than in the UK (60 per cent), while ability and knowledge tests seemed somewhat more commonly used (50 per cent). Situational or work sample tests were also relatively common (37 per cent) while both projective tests and graphology were rarely used (6 per cent). A comparison of Belgian practice shows a wide divide between Flemish and Wallonian regions. A range of selection methods are used in both parts of the country, and both cultures make extensive use of application forms and less use of references as compared to the UK. Flemish companies, however, are much more likely to use personality and cognitive tests than Wallonian companies. Wallonian companies in contrast were much more likely to use graphology, resembling French companies in this respect (Shackleton and Newell, 1994). Both Belgian regions appear to use a mixture of one-to-one and panel interviews involving line managers and personnel managers, though Flemish companies were also often likely to include a consultant.

Netherlands

Altink *et al.* (1991) looked at selection practices in the Netherlands. They found that application forms and interviews were widely used, and that more than half of the larger companies surveyed used medical examinations, psychological tests and references. Graphology was infrequently used. Much selection work was handled by psychologists, an apparently growing trend.

Italy

Italian companies appear to make the least use of alternative selection methods to the interview, even using application forms and references less than other European countries. Other methods are rarely used. The interview itself often involves line managers rather than personnel managers and there are often a series of interviews (Shackleton and Newell, 1994).

France

Shackleton and Newell (1991) extended their survey to take in French companies. They found that compared to UK companies French companies were more likely to use graphology, cognitive tests, one-to-one interviews and serial interviews for the selection of managers. They were less likely to use biodata, references, assessment centres, panel interviews or personality tests. In both countries the interview remained by far the most common technique. Clarke (1993) also found that French recruitment consultancies made much greater use of graphology than recruitment consultancies in other countries.

Australia

Australia shows a similar pattern of assessment to the UK (di Millia *et al.*, 1994). The business sector in Australia seems to make greater use of cognitive testing and assessment centres than manufacturing, retail or government. The government sector made more use of application forms and panel interviews.

Greece

Papalexandris (1991) looked at human resource practices in Greece, and compared Greek companies with foreign-owned subsidiaries. For Greek companies, the main source of new recruits was 'people belonging to the firm's immediate surroundings'. These include friends and family of employees. Only when these avenues proved fruitless were other sources explored. Foreign firms operating in Greece made more use of advertising and personnel consultancy firms in recruitment. For all firms, academic qualifications were important, but these could be waived in favour of 'contacts'. All firms operating in Greece placed importance on the interview, but foreign firms added personality, intelligence and achievement tests to their selection procedures.

Germany

Shackleton and Newell (1994) also surveyed selection practices in Germany, albeit on a smaller scale than their UK and French studies. They found that in Germany interviews, application forms, references and aptitude tests were most commonly used. Panel interviews involving both personnel and line managers seem also common. Assessment centres were less frequently used than in the UK, being most commonly used for graduate recruits and for senior appointments. Psychometric tests were also less common, and German respondents seemed to be more sceptical about their reliability and validity. They were also less likely than British respondents to value the qualifications of the test user or to see test user training as important; less likely to see the feedback of results to candidates as important; and more likely to feel constrained by the legal rights invested in employees, such as rights to dignity and privacy. They appeared under greater pressure to seek the applicant's consent to any procedures, as expressed through the relevant Works Council. In general, German HRM practice does not appear to resemble the proactive, strategic model recommended by US textbooks, being much narrower and more oriented towards legal rules, regulations and formal agreements. Schuler *et al.* (1991) found that application forms, medical examinations and interviews were generally used, while psychological tests used were often clinical in orientation. The use of graphology seemed to be declining.

USA

Ryan and Sackett (1987) found that 83 per cent of organizational psychologists used some form of personal history form, suggesting that the application form is still a major source of information.

Seventy-eight per cent of those surveyed used ability tests and personality inventories, with simulation exercises used by 38 per cent. Clinical or Projective tests were used by 34 per cent of organizations. The most widely used technique was the interview, with 94 per cent of respondents using the method for all assessments. Other surveys have shown that reference checks, unstructured interviews and work samples are much more frequently used in the USA than assessment centres, personality tests or cognitive ability tests (Rowe *et al.*, 1994).

Canada

Personnel legislation in Canada exists at both provincial and federal levels. Aptitude tests in a 1993 survey were used by 50 per cent of organizations, personality tests by 33 per cent, work samples by 31 per cent, assessment centres by 16 per cent, interest inventories by 14 per cent and honesty testing by 1 per cent of organizations surveyed (Thacker and Caltaneo, 1993). Ninety-nine per cent of organizations used interviews.

Managing diversity in selection and assessment practices

It is tempting to speculate on some of the reasons for these national differences. It may be that work on cultural differences by Hofstede (1980) casts some light on this issue. For example, France appears to be a culture showing much higher levels of both uncertainty avoidance and power distance than the USA or UK. It may be that French companies use serial interviews to progressively obtain the approval of superiors, in line with their preference for 'high power distance', and also seek to reduce risks and uncertainty, in line with their high 'uncertainty avoidance'. The Germans, too, show high 'uncertainty avoidance', seeking to reduce ambiguity by reliance on formal, written collective laws, regulations and procedures. However, such an analysis is clearly only partly helpful in explaining the differences observed in national selection practice. For example, Francophone (Wallonian) Belgian companies are like French companies in their use of graphology and unlike Flemish (Dutch) Belgian companies in this respect. However, whereas Belgium scores even more highly than France on 'uncertainty avoidance', its use of graphology does not approach that of France, even in Wallonia. In addition, 'uncertainty avoidance' does not seem to be associated with the number of techniques used (Shackleton and Newell, 1994). Whereas German companies resemble British companies in their much greater use of assessment centres than is the practice in most other European countries, they are unlike British companies and more like Italian companies in their distaste for psychological tests. This suggests that, in addition to general cultural influences, specific intellectual and scientific traditions also influence selection practice. The influence of organizational psychologists as a profession seems to also be relevant, with their influence being much stronger in Flanders than in Italy or France. The influence of the legal and regulatory framework and the nature of any industrial relations codes of practice seems also very influential, since in Germany there is a need to obtain applicant consent for the use of graphology or psychometric tests. As Shackleton and Newell (1994) point out, such differences become important in a Europe increasingly moving towards harmonization in its business methods and employment practices. This wide diversity may cause confusion and frustrate the expectations of other country nationals seeking employment in a particular country.

Fairness, diversity and equality in assessment practice

Another area where applicant diversity is an issue and where the social process model has focused considerable research efforts is equality. From this perspective, equal opportunity considerations enter into every stage and phase of the recruitment, assessment and selection process. Such considerations are not marginal 'extras' to the design, implementation and evaluation of such processes but are built into every phase. For example, forecasting human resource needs could reflect equal opportunity concerns by monitoring the representation of staff at all levels according to gender, race and ethnicity, disability and age.

Under-representation of specific groups identified by an equal opportunity audit – such as people from ethnic minority groups or women in managerial jobs – may then generate targeted recruitment programmes to actively recruit or develop such categories for consideration for promotion (Iles and Auluck, 1991). Such positive action programmes are permissible under existing UK equality legislation, but discrimination – positive or negative – at the point of selection is not. Several codes of practice, influenced by this model, offer prescriptions as to how assessment should be conducted in practice.

Equal opportunity considerations also affect the chain of events from job analysis to the evaluation of effectiveness. Job analysis – identifying critical job tasks and the personal attributes required to perform the job – often involves mostly able-bodied white male samples, especially for managerial jobs, and may not pick up other ways of being 'effective' in the job. As far as is feasible, care should be taken to ensure that as wide a range of groups as possible is sampled. Similarly, the job description needs to be checked to ensure that it does include relevant tasks, and the personnel specification monitored for both omission of relevant attributes and inclusion of non-relevant ones. Existing British equality legislation permits the use of gender or race as a 'genuine occupational qualification' in some circumstances – such as those where a personal service to particular groups is required and where the service is most appropriately carried out by a member of that group.

In these cases, consultation with relevant bodies such as the Commission for Racial Equality or the Equal Opportunities Commission would be advisable, as would the categorization of attributes listed in the personnel specification into 'essential' and 'desirable'. Relevant British Equality legislation not only makes direct discrimination illegal (that is, the less favourable treatment of a person on non-job relevant grounds); it also makes *indirect* discrimination illegal. This is defined as the setting of conditions or requirements which, though in theory are open to all categories, in practice disadvantage some groups in ways that cannot be justified on job-relevant grounds. This consideration is particularly relevant at the personnel specification and assessment and selection stages so as to avoid 'adverse impact' or disproportionate and unjustifiable rejection of specific groups. Similarly, the actual outcomes of selection and placement decisions need to be monitored and evaluated from an equal opportunity perspective, both in terms of the performance criteria chosen to validate procedures and in terms of the comparable hiring rates of specific groups. Increasingly, European Union equality legislation has had an impact on UK personnel practice, especially in terms of equal pay, marital status and sexual harassment. Specific legislation, modelled more firmly on American 'affirmative action' approaches to actively promote more equal representation and targeted particularly on religious background, is present in Northern Ireland. British equality laws may move further in this direction and age, disability and sexual orientation issues may also be pushed higher up the agenda for legislative action.

Many American studies of selection and assessment practices until the late 1980s tended to show evidence of race effects in selection and assessment. These findings were often based on experimental simulations with student raters rather than on real life studies of actual managers. They also tended to focus on black-white comparisons rather than examine a wider range of ethnic groups. However, more recent studies have shown much less discrimination, perhaps due to the influence of equal opportunity and affirmative action legislation. The widespread existence of ethnic and gender stereotypes however has stimulated many of the recent moves towards 'managing diversity' in the USA, training managers to value differences rather than disparage them as deficient as judged by white male norms, and so manage multicultural organizations more effectively (e.g. Auluck and Iles, 1994; Braich and Iles, 1994).

In the UK, evidence of substantial racial discrimination in recruitment and selection, both overt and covert, helped lead to the passage of Race Relations Acts in 1968 and 1975. However, substantial discrimination has been noted many years after the passage of legislation outlawing both direct and indirect discrimination. For example, Brown and Gay (1985) showed that black applicants of similar educational background and qualifications were less likely to be called for interviews for mainly clerical and white-collar jobs, while more recent investigations by the Commission for Racial Equality have uncovered substantial discrimination against black accountants and lawyers (e.g. Iles and Auluck, 1991).

With regard to selection techniques themselves, recent concern has been shown over a number of cases in the UK where psychometric tests have been employed in such a way as to have an 'adverse impact' on black applicants. For example, London Underground in 1988 used such tests to select for middle managers from existing staff. Around 30 per cent of applicants of ethnic minorities applied, very similar to their proportion in the work force, and a similar percentage was shortlisted on the basis of their application forms. However, only 11 per cent were subsequently offered jobs on the basis of a structured interview and cognitive and personality tests (Commission for Racial Equality, 1990). Two firms of occupational psychologists disagreed as to whether the tests matched selection requirements, were at the right level, or were valid as predictors of job success for ethnic minorities as well as white staff (Feltham and Smith, 1993). On the basis of these findings and allegations of unlawful discrimination, London Underground admitted to the charges of unlawful discrimination and revised its selection procedures.

While the response of some organizations to such findings has been to abandon psychometric testing altogether, or to use it to set very low cut-off points, other organizations have responded differently. Some have attempted to demonstrate that such tests *do* show content, construct and criteria-related validity – a procedure long recommended by psychologists as good practice anyway. In particular, psychologists have recommended that studies be carried out for what is called 'differential validity' – that is, the possibility that test scores predict quite differently for different subgroups, such as African-Americans or Hispanics. Other strategies sometimes recommended include:

- providing minorities and/or all groups practice in test taking
- providing extra coaching in test taking
- checking test items for bias, using teams composed of representatives from the various groups involved
- trialling tests with minority groups
- checking for item bias in evaluating trial results

- standardizing the tests with representatives of the various communities for which the test is intended included.

Feltham and Smith (1993) give a good recent account, from a British perspective, of some of these issues.

An alternative strategy, pursued in the USA in particular in response to the legal and political challenges to testing, is to develop procedures which are as valid predictors as tests and also fairer to minorities and women, involving less adverse impact. In general, such alternative procedures such as assessment centres or work samples may also be more acceptable to candidates from all backgrounds. However, there is some concern that formalization of procedures – comprehensive job analyses, structured interview guides, meticulous record keeping, and the like – may not actually promote equal opportunities, but may be used by selectors to mask discrimination or legitimate and justify it. The 'formalization' model, in its unitarist, conflict-free, and apolitical model of organizational life, may not therefore in practice actually advance equality. This is an issue we take up in more detail in Chapter 5, which focuses on the perspective on assessment derived from critical theory.

Recruiting non-traditional workers

One strategy to increase the effectiveness and equity of recruitment is to direct efforts towards less common and/or less traditional sources of applicants. This may not lead to lower quality applicants or the lowering of standards, as there is considerable evidence of discrimination against women and people from ethnic minority groups on grounds *not* related to job performance, as well as evidence that female managers may have higher qualifications than male managers yet enjoy lower pay rates. Many British children of minority ethnic background have higher levels of educational qualifications than comparable white children, yet are less favourably employed. For example, studies in the UK using applicants matched for qualifications and experience but differing in ethnic background showed that applicants from Afro-Caribbean and Asian backgrounds had much more difficulty in obtaining interviews or in securing job offers (Iles

Box 4.1

Rank Xerox (UK) Ltd, having established an equal opportunities
policy, undertook a programme of positive action advertising in
the 1990s, partly as a response to recruitment difficulties and partly
to break down sex segregation in its work force. The recruitment of
customer response controllers, who were traditionally female, was
proving increasingly difficult in Milton Keynes. Rank Xerox employed gender-balanced advertisement visuals and text showing
both men and women in the role, with the phrase 'we only discriminate on ability'. Advertisements made it clear that although
the company was interested in recruiting more men, it was also
keen on receiving applications from equally qualified women. The
advertisement succeeded in attracting more applicants from both
men *and* women.

The insurance firm Prudential Assurance, also active in the equal
opportunities area, designed and implemented similar recruitment
programmes aimed at attracting more women returners and
people from ethnic minority groups to sales roles. Advertisements
provided balanced text and visuals and focused on the openness of
posts to everyone. Interestingly, women and ethnic minorities are
increasingly being targeted as customers in this sector, thereby
providing a link between this initiative and the company's changing market place. Following the advertisement, applications
generally increased, particularly from women and ethnic minorities, and white males did not seem to be deterred from applying.

Finally, the independent UK television company Channel 4 has
attempted to integrate people with disabilities into all aspects of its
programming, via permanent jobs and a special two-year training
programme linking college courses with placements.

(*Source:* Paddisan, 1990)

and Auluck, 1991). Similarly, women may be particularly discri-
minated against when applying for 'non-traditional' jobs such as
managerial ones, despite evidence that women managers in the
UK tend to be better qualified than their male counterparts
(Alban-Metcalfe and Nicholson, 1984). Applicants from 'non-
traditional' pools may therefore not in fact be less qualified or
competent, despite the prejudices and stereotypes held by many
employers.

However, organizations may need to make significant changes to their HRM practices if they are to reflect good HRM practice, and this can also benefit employees from traditional sources, such as white males. Changes in selection, training and career development practices may need to be implemented if an equal opportunities policy is to be fully realized, not just changes in recruitment practices. Flexible working and child-care arrangements may also be necessary to attract atypical applications, as Box 4.1 shows.

In order to attract 'non-traditional' employees, such as people from ethnic minorities, people with disabilities or women returners, a variety of changes in recruitment and assessment practice might be needed. Such approaches could include the following actions from an employer:

- stating that it is striving to be an equal opportunities employer
- stating that it positively welcomes such applicants
- using photographs of such groups in a variety of jobs in recruitment literature; including representatives from such groups in talks, presentations, videos, brochures, interviews; including pen-portraits of 'typical careers' from representatives of such groups
- advertising vacancies in new sources, e.g. in the ethnic minority press, women's press, local radio, community centres, and not just in national newspapers and journals or conventional trade or professional journals
- placing advertisements in minority languages
- making contact with girls' as well as boys' schools, with inner-city colleges as well as with rural universities, and with inner-city comprehensive schools as well as with maintained or private schools
- emphasizing flexible hours, crèches or career-break schemes
- examining the person specification to ensure that the criteria stated (such as educational qualifications, mobility) are in fact necessary and do not discriminate indirectly against particular groups
- reviewing the person specification with regard to the inclusion of such attributes as knowledge of community languages, cultures or market preferences

- training recruiters in equal opportunities so as to avoid off-putting and perhaps discriminatory and illegal signals, messages and questions.

Experience of targeted recruitment indicates that it is effective, stimulating applications from the targeted group without deterring traditional applicants, but that it needs careful planning and expert advice to avoid legal pitfalls. In addition, selectors need training at all levels, from gatekeepers and receptionists through to interviewers. Follow-up action in the form of reviews of induction, training, development and work practices and organizational culture will also be necessary. However, such training is likely to improve the effectiveness of recruitment, training and induction generally, not just for specific groups.

For example, the National Association for the Care and Re-settlement of Offenders (NACRO) began to develop equal opportunities (EO) policies in relation to both employment and service provision in 1982. A code of practice was adopted in 1985, with rules on recruitment, career development, complaints and working conditions. All job descriptions include EO responsibilities and all person specifications include EO commitment. The emphasis has been on integrating EO policy into mainstream activities and practice.

Greater London Citizens Advice Bureau Services Ltd (GLCABS) had also had an EO policy since 1982, with a commitment to positive action in recruitment and training and to 'service accessibility' for all groups. A code of practice in recruitment and selection was implemented in 1986. Although increasing the number of workers from ethnic minorities did seem to increase the number of clients from ethnic minorities using the service, thus making it more 'accessible', the service delivery aspects were seen as having less priority than the employment aspects (Paton and Hooker, 1990).

Women in management and assessment practice

Despite many years of equal opportunity legislation in the UK and USA, the percentage of women in senior management positions remains very low in both countries at less than 5 per cent (Hirsh and Jackson, 1990; Powell, 1993). This is despite the increasing participation of women in the work force generally, and even in the ranks of junior and middle management (women make up 42 per cent of the management work force in the USA, according to Powell, 1993). In the UK, women managers are most numerous in service organizations and in public service organizations, but even here they are greatly under-represented in senior management roles. This is not due to lower achievement motivation or lack of qualifications; two large-scale studies of women managers by Davidson and Cooper (1984) and Alban-Metcalfe and Nicholson (1984) showed that they had equivalent or superior qualifications, expressed similar work preferences to men (though rating intrinsic factors such as job challenge and autonomy more highly) and saw themselves as equally creative, confident and ambitious. They were, however, less likely to be married and less likely to have children than equivalent male managers, suggesting that they had to overcome or forego competing domestic demands more often than male managers. They also reported more stressors than similarly placed men, including stresses associated with career/non-career conflicts and from the masculine cultures of most work environments. These included exclusion, not being taken seriously, and a lack of development opportunities. They also faced considerable pressures to perform and conform to primarily male organizational cultures and values (Marshall, 1984). Such a scenario has given rise to much speculation (and some research) in both the UK and the USA on the 'glass ceiling' held to prevent or make difficult the rise of women (and ethnic minorities) beyond certain organizational levels (e.g. Morrison and von Glinow, 1990; Davidson and Cooper, 1992).

One set of practices which may be contributing to this situation are the recruitment, selection and assessment practices which mark the 'boundary passages' that all employees must make. The criteria used in organizational recruitment, selection and assessment, whether formally derived through job-analysis procedures like repertory grids or critical incidents or (more commonly) subjectively derived on the basis of managers' intuitions as to what makes a 'good employee', are likely to be derived from white male samples. They may reflect the kinds of skills and qualities traditionally associated with white males, such as objectivity, competitiveness and rationality, just as modes of career progression reflect male patterns of continuous employment, high workload, frequent job changes and relocations, and strict age timetables. Such characteristics as teamwork, participation and empowerment may, however, be becoming increasingly relevant as organizations devolve, flatten and institute multi-skilled, self-directed team systems. Such characteristics appear to be more commonly associated with female management styles (Rosener, 1990), suggesting that traditional views of what makes for organizational success may have to be revised.

In addition, many studies of the way selection procedures operate in practice have shown that interviews, with their reliance on subjective opinion, systematically discriminate against women when applying for traditionally masculine jobs, such as management or engineering. Newer, apparently more 'objective' techniques such as biodata, in their reliance on past behaviour linked to successful performance, may also discriminate against women, as may the use of personality inventories based on primarily male norms and samples. The group exercises used in assessment centres may also disadvantage women, since women (and black people) are often a minority in such groups. Much socio-psychological research has demonstrated that in such situations female leadership activity is considerably reduced, with restrictions on their opportunities for input and frequent interruptions or ignoring of female contributions by male participants. The assessors, often male line managers, may also hold stereotypical views of women. As Schein (1973, 1978, 1989) found, 'to think manager is to think male', certainly for British, German and US male managers, if not now for US women managers. I observed a British building society assessment centre where a women's assertive competitive performance – qualities the assessor claimed to be looking for – was seen as the 'aggressive zapping of people' (Mabey and Iles, 1993). Other research on assessment has shown that performance of the same task to the same standard may be attributed differently according to gender by observers – 'what's skill for the male is luck for the female', as Deaux and Emswiller (1974) put it. Research on British managers' responses to diversity suggests similar attribution processes may operate to the detriment of Black women in particular (Braich and Iles, 1994). This means that even successful task performance by women may be attributed less to competence or skill and more to luck or task ease. Task failure may be attributed to low ability for women, but to bad luck for men. Women performing well in traditionally 'feminine' tasks, however, may be rated more positively than men performing such tasks to the same standard (Braich and Iles, 1994).

Similar effects, often interacting with gender, have been noted with regard also to race. Black American women have been noted as receiving lower ratings in an assessment centre as the number of white men in their assessment group rose (Schmidt and Hill, 1977). Other studies of gender and assessment centres have, however, failed to detect any differences in the overall ratings of males and females (Iles, 1990).

Assessment processes as social processes

Much of the preceding analysis has been based on a rational model of decision making. Organizational strategy is seen as determined by systematic assessment of external opportunities and threats and internal strengths and weaknesses. The implications of this for organizational structure are noted and careful consideration is given to the roles that employees will need to play and to the skills and attributes they will need to display. Recruitment and formal assessment and appraisal can then be carried out against objective criteria that are clearly and demonstrably related to job-related skills and relevant job performance and success. Selection and promotion decisions can then be taken in a way that avoids subjectivity, prejudice and bias. Most textbooks on personnel management or selection and assessment recommend the adoption of just such a formalized, systematic, rational and objective model of assessment and selection process, though usually downplaying or ignoring the strategic aspects.

However, organizational decision making in practice departs in many respects from this ideal and presents an altogether more political and informal set of processes. Furthermore, this model of rational assessment against objective criteria is vulnerable and has been increasingly challenged from a number of directions, such as how significant individual differences are to overall organizational performance, how stable and persistent such differences are, how reliable is the measurement of particular assessment criteria, how neutral assessment procedures are, the value of the criteria used to validate selection decisions, the role of power and control in the selection process, and the dominance of the psychometric paradigm. These challenges have mainly come from, and have contributed to, the social process and critical perspectives.

The emerging European social process perspective

Our earlier consideration of the German selection context in particular demonstrates the sensitivity of European selection practice to considerations of the rights of the applicant to *dignity, privacy and information* and the importance placed on applicant consent and active participation in the process. This concern is also manifested in the practice of other European countries, such as the Netherlands (e.g. de Wolff and Van den Bosch, 1984). It also shows up in a stream of European research on selection and assessment as social processes (e.g. Iles *et al.*, 1989; Fletcher, 1991; Robertson *et al.*, 1991, de Witte *et al.*, 1992; Iles and Robertson, 1997). For example, Iles and Robertson (1989, 1997) have presented a theoretical model of the impact of selection and assessment processes on individuals, arguing that both the selection decision and candidate's attitudes to the selection process are likely to have effects on a variety of psychological processes including organizational and career attitudes, self-efficacy, self-esteem and psychological states, and these are likely to lead to such behaviours as job and career withdrawal.

The impact of such processes is likely to be moderated by a variety of factors, such as candidate individual differences, prior information and explanation, features of the assessment process such as the quality, quantity and timing of any feedback, and contextual variables such as the amount of organizational and social support provided to candidates. Partial support was provided for the model by empirical studies of development centres and assessment procedures in UK financial services organizations. Participants in a UK clearing bank's fast-track management development programme perceived the fairness, accuracy and adequacy of the assessment techniques used in the programme (biodata, situational interviews and assessment centres) very differently, and their perceptions were influenced by whether they were judged to have passed or failed the procedure. In general, participants viewed assessment centres more positively, and were more likely to react positively to procedures if selected by them. In early career stage candidates' post-assessment commitment to their organization was primarily related to the perceived career impact of the procedure. In later career stages commitment was more related to the perceived adequacy of the procedure (Robertson et al., 1991). Other British studies have shown that assessment centre failure may lead to lower self-esteem and need for achievement (Fletcher, 1991), and that development centre participation can affect career plans and attitudes (Iles et al., 1989).

This emerging 'social process' model of assessment being developed in Europe makes several assumptions which contrast with those underlying the US psychometric model. One is that people do change constantly in the course of their careers in organizations. This assumption underlies much of the British work on career and work-role transitions (Nicholson, 1984), as well as providing much of the impetus to European training and development work which often make extensive use of action learning and work-based learning. Another assumption, in contrast to the US model, is that subjective self-perceptions are critical to people's work motivation and performance, and that these are influenced by assessment and selection procedures. The jobs people do increasingly involve interaction, negotiation and mutual influence, often taking place in multi-skilled, flexible, self-directed work teams. This emphasis on negotiation, interaction and mutual influence is perhaps one reason why European organizations continue to rely on the interview as the main selection method, as it opens up opportunities for bilateral exchange of views, mutual decision making and mutual negotiation. In addition, the recognition that assessment processes are social processes is particularly appropriate to the role of assessment in facilitating *development*, whether individual or organizational development.

In this social process model of assessment, individuals are expected to provide information to the organization on abilities, expectations, aspirations, life history and other relevant attributes. They will expect to be provided with information by the organization on its culture and on the nature of the jobs and careers available, as well as information and feedback on the results of tests or assessments conducted by it. Both the individual and the organization will expect to make decisions on the basis of the information each has received, to assess the suitability for each party of the contracts being entered into (legal and psychological), negotiate on their terms and make decisions (Herriot, 1993).

Some recent US research into the impact of selection and assessment techniques, perhaps stimulated by this stream of European research, has also looked to social psychology to examine assessment processes. One such stream has examined the interview as a process of interaction, examining the role of such variables as non-verbal behaviour, age, disability, appearance, gender, race and physical attractiveness on interviewers' ratings, though often in the acontextual, ahistorical ways characteristic of individualistic US social psychology. Often employing students as 'interviewers' and using 'paper people' consisting of CVs and photographs, it has also often used brief taped transcripts of interviews (e.g. Heilman and Stopeck, 1985; Herriot, 1987; Powell, 1990). British research in this tradition has been more likely to employ real life recruiters and candidates (e.g. Iles, 1991). In this particular study a bank's assessment centre ratings were in general not related to ratings of appearance, physical attractiveness, or gender, in contrast to the results obtained in many US laboratory interview studies. Salaman and Thompson (1978) have also shown how selection procedures in the Army, while ostensibly 'objective' rely on a whole set of class-based stereotypes and biases.

Another perspective drawn from US social psychological studies of the legal process has been to differentiate *procedural* from *distributive* justice. Distributive justice refers to the perceived fairness of the outcome or result (in an HRM context, was the size of the pay rise or the outcome of the selection decision or appraisal fair?) while procedural justice refers to the perceived fairness of the means or procedures used to determine the result (e.g. the perceived fairness of the reward, appraisal or selection process). Though distributive justice has been shown to be influential in determining some reactions, such as satisfaction with pay rises, procedural justice appears to be more influential in influencing organizational commitment and trust in management. It appears that similar dynamics operate in the selection and assessment field, and that procedural justice feelings are generated by such features of the assessment process as having prior information, receiving adequate explanations, having recourse to appeals or challenges, getting feedback, being treated in a courteous, unbiased professional way, and being assessed in job-related ways (Iles and Robertson, 1997).

More fundamental challenges to the dominant psychometric perspective have come from critical theory and sociology. After reviewing some of the major challenges posed to the classical model, we will go on to discuss a particular approach in critical theory deriving from Michel Foucault, which places selection firmly in the context of knowledge and power in organizations.

5

A DISCOURSE PERSPECTIVE

A number of challenges have been made to the classical, psychometrically influenced model of selection and assessment. These include considerations of the following:

The significance of the contribution of individual difference to organizational performance

The classical model assumes that individual differences in performance contribute significantly to organizational effectiveness. However, organizational performance is affected by many other factors apart from individual skills and abilities, including variables related to individual differences in motivation and style, variables relating to leadership and supervision, and variables relating to the structure and culture of the organization as a whole.

The stability and permanence of individual differences

The psychometric model assumes that individual differences are relatively stable and permanent. However, much research has shown that these differences are *not* necessarily permanent and stable, but malleable and open to change, and indeed are often directly affected by subsequent work experiences. The psycho-metric model assumes that individual differences can be mea-sured independently of each other and change little over time.

The reliability of measurement of particular assessment criteria

Some authors such as Jacobs (1989) have argued that certain 'soft' skills and competencies, such as creativity and sensitivity, often regarded as being crucial to successful job performance in turbu-lent conditions and a feature of many assessment centres, cannot be reliably measured, certainly not under the simulation scen-arios employed in assessment centre designs. However, others argue that such criteria can be reliably measured in simulations and at work (Cockerill, 1989) or, if not in simulations, then through psychometric methods such as personality tests (Dule-wicz, 1989).

The 'neutrality' of selection and assessment instrument

The classical model assumes that selection procedures are neutral measuring instruments, assessing psychological characteristics without discernible psychological impact on the subject being measured. However, this seems an invalid assumption as some selection instruments are much more positively regarded than others and have different impacts on individuals' work experi-ences (Iles and Robertson, 1989, 1997). The significance of this is that the perceived adequacy of the procedure can impact posi-tively or negatively on employees' commitment to their work.

The power of the organization in the assessment process

In continental Europe in particular, the prevailing model of as-sessment and selection has been criticized for neglecting appli-cants' rights to privacy and for putting them in a position of disadvantage and powerlessness (de Wolff and van den Bosch, 1984). These criticisms have led to recommendations on data protection, on privacy and confidentiality, on fairness and on appeals, as well as an emphasis on the rights of both parties to the process to adequate and relevant information. For example, there are legal restrictions on what German employers can ask of candidates, and works councils in Germany may see selection as being within their sphere of influence and approval (Newell and Shackleton, 1992). The applicant's consent to testing, for example, needs to be obtained, which may in part account for the lower use of psychometric tests in Germany. The psychometric model assumes that selection is by the organization, not by the applicant.

The criteria used to validate selection decisions

The classical model assumes that the criteria needed to validate the accuracy of predictions made by selection procedures can be measured, typically in terms of individuals' contributions to the organization. Apparently 'objective' criteria in fact depend on a series of subjective judgements. Researchers and practitioners often judge the success of selection procedures primarily in terms of productivity or economic contribution, rather than in terms of other criteria such as individual well-being, the meeting of personal expectations or social contribution. Indeed, utility theory makes the primacy of economic criteria fully explicit. A number of other criteria, such as bias and acceptability, could also be used. Psychometric psychology assumes that work is performed by individuals, through grouping tasks into jobs which are also relatively stable, and that job performance is both measurable and attributable to individuals.

The control of the selection process

Studies of recruitment practices suggest that personnel managers are often too remote or too engrossed in subordinate, servicing roles to ensure that formal, structured selection practices are properly implemented. Local line managers are often able to resist attempts to make informal practices more structured and formal, seeing them as bureaucratic, costly, time consuming, a diversion to the main business and as challenging their own autonomy and prerogatives. Such attitudes may result in the recruitment of 'traditional', stereotypical candidates.

103

The dominance of particular professional paradigms

Before the rise of the 'classical' model, the trend in continental Europe was towards clinical and intuitive approaches that stressed the value of professional judgement, personal contact, projective tests and qualitative assessment. The 'success' of psychometric testing in mass selection during two world wars, especially in the United States of America, challenged this paradigm, replacing it with the statistical, rational, objective model. This in turn came under fire in the USA, in particular in the late 1960s and early 1970s, for its alleged cultural, racial and gender bias. In the 1980s, it re-emerged as the dominant model, with the decade witnessing a phenomenal growth in the popularity of psychometric tests of personality as well as of ability. In the 1990s, there appears to be a trend towards more collaborative, participative and negotiated assessment procedures, as embodied in the movements away from assessment centres and towards development centres, joint appraisal and the employment of psychometric tests with feedback. The psychometric model assumes that the main purpose of assessment is the prediction of job performance, which will lead to better organizational performance.

One can see at least a partial move in the 1990s towards more collaborative assessment and planning, more active participation by the assessee, more attention given to the assessee's views, more ownership of the data by the assessee, and greater focus on the needs of the assessee. However, assessment, and especially development, centres are used primarily in situations where both participant and assessor come from similar, relatively powerful social groups and where the 'clients' – especially senior managers – have the economic, social and political power to influence the terms of the exchange.

The tendency of assessment practitioners to deal very differently with diverse social groups is illustrated in Zimbabwe, where psychometric tests were used to provide individual help and guidance for white children, but to select rigorously on a mass basis the 15 per cent of African children granted access to secondary education – that is to serve administrative, and ultimately political, purposes (Hollway, 1991).

Much has been made recently of moves towards the 'flexible firm' (Atkinson, 1984; Pollert, 1988) where the employment status of workers is increasingly differentiated. A primary core may enjoy full-time relatively secure and well-paid employment in return for increased functional flexibility and multi-skilling; more peripheral, secondary or distanced workers – part-time, temporary, sub-contracted, agency, consultancy and out-sourced workers – may not enjoy such benefits.

Unskilled 'peripheral' workers may receive little assessment; skilled peripheral workers may be treated to standardized tests of performance and ability to select them for specific jobs; core workers, especially senior managers, may be treated to the full gamut of sensitive, extensive collaborative assessment – psychometric testing with feedback and participative development centres. Feedback, counselling, joint goal-setting and action planning, with many training and development resources targeted towards this group alone may also be increasing features of assessment practices. Such considerations require us to pay more attention to more critical approaches to selection and assessment.

As we have seen, in Chapter 3 in particular, selection and assessment research and practice in the UK has been heavily influenced by the 'psychometric' model most fully developed in the USA. This model in a variety of forms is represented in most textbooks of HRM, personnel management and organization psychology as 'good professional practice', if not fully represented in actual practice. The model has its roots in nineteenth- and early twentieth-century British work on individual differences and in the development of sophisticated psychometric and statistical techniques. Its paradigm status in work psychology and personnel management owes much of its application to mass vocational selection in the USA in both world wars. Its principal focus is the 'job', conceived of as a set of discrete tasks. In this model, performance criteria are selected and individual 'attributes' of various kinds (knowledge, skills, abilities, etc.) are chosen as predictors of job performance. The attributes selected are then measured through a variety of procedures (tests, interviews, biodata, etc.) and the assessment process validated primarily in terms of criteria-related predictive validity (how well the predictor actually predicts job performance), usually expressed as a correlation coefficient. Other validity dimensions (e.g. construct, content validity) are also sometimes considered. This model appears to place a high value on individualism (individual attributes are taken to predict individual performance), managerialism (the major criteria of performance are the achievement of organizational goals as defined by top management) and utility (cost-benefit analysis of the monetary benefits conferred on organizations in using different selection procedures). Other concerns such as bias or adverse impact on women and minorities may also be taken into account. Recent developments in utility theory in assessing the benefits of investing in good selection practice are often attempted, so as to give psychologists and personnel practitioners an equal say in the 'language of business' to other business professionals (Herriot, 1993).

However, this model rests on a number of assumptions that are open to challenge. One is that by and large people do not change much – the characteristics they display before assessment remain quite stable, which is why prediction of job performance is possible. It also assumes that objective assessment of individual attributes is possible, and that this can be used to predict job performance. In addition, the assumption seems to be that job content also does not change much, and that job content primarily consists of specific sets of tasks which can be identified through job analysis. It also makes the assumption that job performance is measurable, though 'objective' assessments of job performance are often hard to come by and supervisor's evaluations of performances or promotion and salary increases are often used instead. Finally, the central assumption made is that the key purpose of assessment is the prediction of job performance.

Clearly, this model has a number of considerable strengths. Individual differences in performance *do* contribute significantly to differences in organizational performance, a contention underlying much of the growth in HRM in recent years. However, many other factors also affect organizational performance, and it does seem as if people do change as a result of job experiences. The kinds of attributes assessed by psychologists – for example, locus of control, self-directedness, intellectual flexibility – do seem to be affected by such work experiences as occupational success, racial discrimination, and the kinds of jobs one performs (e.g. Iles and Robertson, 1995).

A variety of factors are causing many researchers and practitioners, especially in Western Europe, to question fundamental aspects of this model. As organizations change, decentralize, restructure, get flatter, and devolve accountability, the conception of the 'job' as a stable collection of discrete tasks has come under pressure (e.g. Atkinson, 1984). Multi-skilling, flexible specialization, and self-directed work teams have made this notion of a 'job' rather outdated, and these and other changes such as downsizing and the growth of 'portfolio careers' have changed our concepts of career success and career development. Knowledge- and skill-based reward systems have also undermined the use of job evaluation and the role of the 'job' as the basis of reward systems (e.g. Luthans and Fox, 1989; Armstrong, 1993). Self-directed work teams, matrix structures and notions of empowerment have challenged the traditional role of the supervisor and the role of supervisor's evaluations, and the increasingly diverse nature of the work force has challenged some of our assumptions about evaluation and the validity of assessment instruments. In addition, in Western Europe assessment has come to play a more strategic role in facilitating individual development and cultural and organizational change, rather than in selection alone (Iles, 1992; Mabey and Iles, 1993).

Another direction to this paradigm of assessment has come from political and legal challenges to the fairness and validity of assessment and selection procedures. In the USA in particular such challenges have come over groups with 'visible differences' such as race, age and gender. Similar concerns, especially with regard to gender but less markedly with regard to age and race have been manifest in recent years in Europe. Civil Rights, feminism, equal employment opportunity and the avoidance of unfair discrimination have become important social values. Assessment instruments have increasingly been seen as exhibiting unfair and illegal discriminatory features. The criterion of 'bias' or 'adverse impact', defined as the degree to which a technique or procedure rejects a disproportionate number of applicants from one social group or screens out group members unfairly in a way that cannot be justified in terms of ability to do the job, has become an increasingly important 'evaluative standard' against which to judge selection procedures. In part this situation led to a drop in the use of psychometric tests in the 1970s; in part it stimulated research into 'validity generalization' to show that tests *were* in fact valid across situations. It also stimulated research into creating selection procedures which were as valid if not more valid than psychometric tests but which generated less 'adverse impact'. Work samples, assessment centres and structured, criteria-related interviews seemed to fit the bill in this respect. All of these procedures display a concern with thorough job analysis to identify the criteria or competencies held to constitute effective job performance and a concern to 'sample' job content directly in the selection procedure itself, in the form of simulations of some kind. This development in itself marks an interesting departure from the traditional psychometric paradigm with its concern to assess rather abstract and general 'signs' as predictors. Traditionally, the predictor 'signs' (rather abstract personality traits or intellectual abilities) are quite remote from actual measures of job performance (Wernimont and Campbell, 1967). In the 'sample' approach, predictor and criteria measures become as close as possible, both representing 'job performance' in some way. Such procedures not only seem less 'biased' than psychometric tests or traditional unstructured interviews; they also seem of similar or even higher validity (Robertson and Iles, 1988).

Reviewing this whole area shows that the research agenda for the psychometric-objective model has not in fact been set by neutral, scientific interests but by political, social and legal pressures. More sophisticated critical adherents to the model (e.g. Hesketh and Robertson, 1993) have called for a clearer conceptual appreciation of the relationships between and among predictors and criteria, and for a better understanding of measurement issues in selection. This position acknowledges that 'the selection literature has been atheoretical, with a primary focus on identifying approaches and techniques that confer practical utility. Comparatively little emphasis has been placed on the development of conceptual framework for selection or on trying to understand why some procedures work and others not' (Hesketh and Robertson, 1993: 3). Their call is for developing a *process* model of selection that places it in a broader theoretical perspective of human abilities, personality, motivation and skill acquisition. Such a model 'also requires an examination of the task demands of environments and their interaction with individual psychological variables' (p. 3). The authors point out that research findings on the assessment centre challenge the construct validity of what is being assessed, with studies showing that ratings tend to cluster according to exercises rather than in terms of the dimensions being assessed. 'This question of what is being measured by these attempts to assess job competence is unresolved and the basis of the validity of such methods is uncertain' (Hesketh and Robertson, 1993: 3).

Selection, power and knowledge

The social process model's critique of traditional psychometric models like the strategic management models described in Chapter 2, tends to complement and incorporate the psychometric model rather than directly challenge its key epistemological and methodological assumptions. Such a challenge comes from critical theory. Drawing on the work of Iles and Salaman (1995), we can view assessment processes in other terms than exploring their efficiency or reasonableness, or in terms of the ways in which reasonableness is constructed and displayed in decision making. Approaches based on the work of Michel Foucault stress the relationship between these processes, the expertise on which they are based, and the practice of power within organizations. Most models of assessment so far discussed take *efficiency* (especially the prediction of productivity) as their primary concern, and focus on ways of improving the efficiency of the processes. They also seek to explain current developments in assessment procedures and criteria in terms of changes in the nature of work organization, such as 'the importance attached to increased individual discretion, and the implications this has for the administration of work' (Townley, 1989: 102).

Foucault, himself a French social theorist, did not apply his approach to HRM but to a range of subjects and social institutions, such as psychiatry, medicine, the human sciences, the penal system and sexuality. His earlier interests were in developing a 'genealogy of knowledge' – that is, how it is that a body of knowledge or subject has been constructed, produced and demarcated from other such bodies. He then became interested in the relationships between knowledge and power, and in the ways seemingly everyday, apparently apolitical practices come to constitute a 'technology of power'.

Unlike many other radical and Marxist approaches to power in organizations, which ask 'who' and 'why' questions about power (e.g. who benefits? why do senior managers act in this way?), Foucauldian approaches tend to focus on 'how' questions, especially how it is that everyday, apparently apolitical HRM procedures such as selection and assessment comprise a 'technology of power', a set of disciplinary practices aimed at making employee behaviour visible, predictable, calculable and manageable (Townley, 1994). Through dividing, partitioning, ordering and ranking procedures such as job evaluation and appraisal, boundaries are imposed and maintained and the work force becomes more manageable. The approach is less concerned with the efficiency or rationality of the perspectives and more concerned with how such boundaries are imposed, maintained and breached, and with what effects. Job analysis and appraisal attempt to coordinate the efforts of employees, while various 'examinatory' techniques such as selection tests and assessment procedures seek to constitute the individual as an object of knowledge and power in order to aid rational decision making. Such procedures act through 'hierarchical observation' and 'normalizing judgement', assuming a set of verifiable, predictable characteristics or competencies in employees and managers. In practice, however, an *image* of management – and a gender and culture specific image at that – is what is being assessed. Psychometric, objective assessment procedures provide a vocabulary and technology that manages individuals in apparently fair, rational and interest-free ways that are divorced from structures of domination and from ethical and political issues. Even procedures such as self-assessment, developmental appraisal, personality inventories with feedback and interviews are seen as acting to actively construct identity and influence how individuals see themselves as employees. These are usually mediated through authority figures or 'confessors' who intervene in order to interpret, judge, punish, forgive and console, such as mentors, consultants or counsellors. Information from such procedures can then become part of an individual's self-understanding, enabling such individuals to reconstitute themselves as productive, enterprising subjects.

Assessment centres as technologies of power

One way of exploring these perhaps rather abstract arguments is through historical examination of the introduction of assessment centres and empirical study of assessment centres in action. Both the social process model and psychometric models of assessment have laid great stress on the need to formalize selection and assessment procedures, not only to enhance reliability and predictive validity but also to reduce unfair discrimination and advance equal opportunities. Proponents of work sample-based methods, like the assessment centre, often contrast them favourably both with psychometric tests and with less structured methods on two grounds: they predict job performance more successfully and they exhibit less adverse impact on minority groups. In this sense, they (and formalized selection practices based on job analysis more generally) provide both a rationale and a technology for anti-discriminatory practices, being seen as fairer, more objective and more rational than both the standard psychometric test and the traditional, unstructured selection interview.

The Foucauldian perspective on assessment centres in contrast focuses less on their validity or utility, and less on efficiency questions on how best to run one, and more on their role as a technology of power, constituting candidates as examinable, observable objects which can be judged against a discourse of the 'ideal worker'. Assessment centres may therefore test merely conformity to the prevailing discourse; a perspective which receives support from findings that assessment centre data are typically validated against supervisor judgements, promotability, career success and salary increases, rather than against 'objective' indices of job success. In many studies, assessment centre ratings are known and used for placement and promotion purposes, leading to 'crown prince' and halo effects – so the high, positive correlation with organizationally defined 'success' is not perhaps surprising. In other studies, where the ratings have been kept from personnel and line managers, high assessment centre ratings may still reflect conformity to a stereotyped model of the 'ideal manager' current in the organization. This is particularly likely to be present when line managers are typically involved in both assessment centre ratings and in subsequent promotion decisions, leading to predictor-criterion contamination; it may not be centre performance itself, but managers' knowledge of that performance, which predicts future promotions.

From a Foucauldian perspective, the development of scientific discourse is seen as critical to the forming of the child, prisoner or employee (Foucault, 1974). The local power of practitioners is closely related to their scientific knowledge and their ability to observe, survey and 'gaze' upon the object of their discourse. This discourse highlights both problems (of irrational decisions, discrimination) and the technology for managing these (assessment centres, tests). Assessment centre technology both defines the norms of acceptable job behaviour (job analysis) and selects candidates who meet standards which reflect that norm. Like the psychiatric and criminological disciplines, it combines the technologies of an observing hierarchy and those of normalizing judgement.

One stream of research into how assessment centres are used in practice emphasizes how they may be used by assessors to 'subvert' formalized selection practices and legitimize or justify informal selection decisions. For example, Salaman and Thompson (1978) showed how the assessment centre scores of working-class and upper-class candidates were differently valued, to the advantage of the upper-class candidate. However, 'all parties insist that they are operating solely on the basis of the formal scientific selection scheme' (p. 286) and centre components 'are used by the officers in their efforts to show the sense, correctness, and inevitability of the selection decisions' (p. 289). Jewson and Mason's (1986, 1987) study of an engineering company also shows that formalized selection procedures may enhance the legitimation rather than the elimination of discrimination, while Knights and Raffo (1990) have shown that the rhetoric of formalized selection can be used to legitimize 'milkround' selection decisions. In addition, assessors may ignore or subvert the formal process either by introducing 'acceptability' criteria such as bearing or appearance in army officer selection (e.g. Vernon and Parry, 1949) or by disregarding assessment centre evidence altogether. For example, Carter's (1996) study of a regional electricity company's use of assessment centres to select distribution managers and team managers in the context of a move from a public sector, bureaucratic, engineering dominated company to a privatized, more entrepreneurial and more commercial one showed that one Network Services Manager (South) made little use of the assessment centre scores, appointing who he wanted. In contrast, the Northern manager selected his distribution and team managers solely on the basis of assessment centre scores, disregarding traditional criteria such as seniority and engineering excellence. Political control over selection decisions is likely to remain resistant to change, and 'non-scientific' judgements are likely to remain in force. However, advanced assessment technology such as assessment centres may be deployed to justify and legitimize such judgements. Line managers and supervisors may resist formalization in order to maintain their own patterns of allegiance and dependency (Jewson and Mason, 1987).

In discussing the social process model, we noted that assessment centres, in contrast to some other technologies such as biodata or psychometric tests, were generally positively regarded by participants. This finding has been noted by early observers of military assessment centres, such as Vernon and Parry (1949: 54): 'time and again, candidates – even failed ones – commented on the fairness, friendliness and thoroughness of the scheme', while Eysenck (1953: 153) noted that 'the selection procedure was considered fair and accurate by most of those who passed through it'. This has also been noted by many reviews of assessment use in business (e.g. Robertson and Iles, 1988) and in many local studies of assessment centre use in financial services organizations (e.g. Robertson et al., 1991). Compared to other techniques, the 'impact validity' of the assessment centre is high, with even failures seeing it as fair, accurate and valid (Iles and Robertson, 1997). However, the significance of this finding has been less often explored from a critical, Foucauldian perspective. Carter (1996) notes that the feedback staff received on their performance in the centre had important implications for how they constituted themselves as employees; successful candidates tended to describe their attributes in terms of such feedback when asked to describe their management style. Successful candidates saw their job of Distribution Manager as vital to the organization, and the old structure as anachronistic. Younger engineers selected for team manager roles welcomed the opportunity; older engineers tended to see it as a demotion. Unsuccessful candidates either accepted redundancy or felt threatened by the negative career prognosis. Many experienced managers chose not to apply, not wanting to be part of the new organization, which surprised the HR department. Many candidates felt that the assessment centre was 'like a game', but nearly all accepted and internalized the judgements made about them, welcoming the centres' apparent openness, structure and fairness in comparison with previous selection methods. The production of knowledge about candidates therefore not only provided the basis for selection decisions, but also the basis for how candidates constituted themselves as managers and employees. The assessment centre also symbolized a cultural break from the past, an epochal shift to a privatized company in a competitive workplace.

Conclusion

In this approach assessment and selection may be regarded as elements in the 'government' of organizations, with a particular focus on the ways in which power, knowledge and practice mutually support and reproduce each other. This is not simply to argue that practices and knowledge support power in an ideological or legitimating manner. Power is that 'which traverses *all* practices – from the "macro" to the "micro" through which persons are ruled, mastered, held in check, administered, steered, guided, by means of which they are led by others or have come to direct or regulate their own actions' (Rose, 1990). Power is thus not located merely in the actions of the State or, within the enterprise, in the actions of senior managers; it is present in all knowledge and practice that regulates individuals, including of course their own. Thus this approach allows us to look for the exercise or practice of power in activities which initially may seem far removed from established centres of power, or removed through the nature and exercise of scientific expertise from the interests and values of the powerful. The processes of assessment and selection are therefore seen as obvious examples of the exercise of power within the detached and scientific process of competence-based, objective, rational assessment (Hollway, 1991).

Power is inherent in knowledge itself, and in the techniques which that knowledge informs and justifies. Knowledge plays a major role in constructing the individual employee as someone calculable, discussible and capable of being comprehended as the subject of senior managerial interventions and decisions. The definition of attributes or competencies may be based on psychometrically informed structures of competence and the process of assessment may be based on psychometrically rigorous testing instruments. These expertises are not simply seen as the servants of power; they *are* power itself, having crucial significance for key decisions about selection, promotion and rejection, and for the characteristics which are defined – and accepted – by all parties as necessary and properly constituting the new manager or 'enterprising employee'. Nor is this their only significance. Competence-based, rational objective assessment also helps to define key assessment qualities while maintaining the necessity and neutrality of these dimensions.

As Hollway has noted, the expertise surrounding the assessment process should be regarded as *produced* rather than discovered (Hollway, 1991: 1). Similarly, the search for managerial competencies has been actively *produced* as a key feature of the process of organizational change and changes in the way employees are managed in organizations.

The processes of selection and assessment offer a striking example from this perspective of a major way in which selectors' actions and judgements on candidates, critical for organizational restructuring and for individual experience, are structured and made rational in terms of expert-derived systems and criteria of selection. Processes of assessment and selection therefore reveal the interrelationships between knowledge and power, demonstrate the ubiquity and diversity of power/knowledge practices, and show the role of a form of organizational governmentality

which allows the exercise of power through calculation, assessment and knowledge. This is seen, from a critical perspective, as
particularly evident in recent discussions of managerial competence, explored more fully in the next chapter.

6

ASSESSMENT AND SELECTION FOR COMPETENCE

Managers are now even more crucial to organizational success than they were, and their role in creating and sustaining competitive advantage is increasingly recognized. Managers are presented with greater responsibilities, demands and pressures as a result of recent changes in organizational environments. These changes are likely to intensify in the future.

Many British organizations have reacted to these challenges by introducing a set of initiatives often labelled 'Human Resource Management' (Salaman *et al.*, 1992; Mabey and Salaman, 1996), including: delayering, decentralization, devolution, downsizing, empowerment initiatives, quality and customer care initiatives, a greater emphasis on entrepreneurship, more use of internal markets, and culture change and performance management initiatives, often accompanied by goal-setting and performance-related pay.

These developments have in turn placed new demands on the (fewer) managers and other employees that remain. Management is increasingly seen as being less about ensuring adherence and compliance to standard procedures, rules and regulations and more about empowering initiative and entrepreneurial behaviour

117

in autonomous employees often working in self-directed teams with high discretion. Organizational and managerial success in the future is likely to be very different from what has been the case in the past, and this is putting pressure on existing models of managerial competence. This requires some exploration of what it is that managers actually do.

Studies of what managers actually do

Standard analyses of how managers spend their time, such as Mintzberg (1973), show us that managers typically work long and hard. These pressures are likely to intensify in the light of the demands of the new managerial work. Managers appear to work in ways that encourage brevity, fragmentation and super-ficiality, preferring instant, oral communication to formal communication channels and eschewing planning and reflection. Indeed, they are 'proficient at superficiality'. This mode of working is not necessarily a result of personal preference. It may also be an outcome generated by the way organizational structures and cultures erect 'barriers to learning' (Salaman and Butler, 1990; Mabey and Iles, 1994).

However, development models built on what managers actually do in the present or have done in the past cannot in themselves help build models that will help managers deal with *future* demands and challenges. For this, we need a conceptual, future-oriented model of what managers should be doing differently to manage well. One area which seems promising in this respect is the study of managerial *competence*, derived from analyses of managerial job content.

A major issue in recruitment and selection in recent years has concerned the process of identifying relevant qualities in existing staff and potential applicants that will enable an appropriate match to occur between the person and the job. These qualities have been variously described as skills, knowledge and other attributes (e.g. personality traits) and are increasingly termed *competences* (UK) or *competencies* (USA). The tool traditionally used to identify relevant attributes has been *job analysis*, regarded as a critical initial stage in the recruitment and selection process.

Job analysis can be divided into *task-oriented* and *person-oriented* methodologies. Task-oriented methodologies generate a list of the activities or tasks required of the job-holder, as derived from observations, diary studies, interviews and surveys.

Job tasks are often rated in conventional job analyses in terms of their importance and frequency. *Task-oriented* analyses are often specific to a particular job and give little information on the skills or qualities needed to do the job adequately; these need to be inferred. Indeed increasingly many staff, such as graduates, are taken on not to do a specific job but to develop a career involving frequent job changes. Recent developments in HRM practice such as flexibility, teamwork and multi-skilling also limit the usefulness of such task-oriented approaches. As a consequence *person-oriented* approaches, such as critical incident, repertory grid and behavioural event interviews have grown in importance as a way of generating more directly the skills and behaviours needed to perform a job (e.g. 'interpersonal skills' as compared to 'chairing meetings').

A principal aim of a job analysis is to generate a *job description*: the job context, its associated tasks, responsibilities and duties. This can then form the basis of the *person specification*, the skills, characteristics and other attributes deemed necessary to do the job. However, conventional job analysis tends to assume that there is such a target as 'the job', defined in terms of a stable collection of discrete tasks, and the knowledge, skills and abilities identified as required for performance are for a job that currently exists. However, in the face of the changes now experienced by organizations (technological change, restructuring, globalization, the growth in a diverse work force, increasing mergers and acquisitions), such assumptions are unlikely to hold.

In addition, many jobs are newly created, with no precedents to fall back on. Conventional job analysis procedures may therefore be historic and backward looking, rather than forward looking and strategic. One alternative is to carry out a *strategic* job analysis, where workshops are held with key employees and other experts to identify future trends and their implications for future skills. This involves such techniques as looking at best practice, examining other sectors, and scenario planning. To take future trends into account, it is necessary to identify what skills will be required of jobs in the future. Information about the future may be collected in a workshop where participants identify the kinds of issues in the job, the organization, and the wider environment that might affect the way the job will go.

It may then be possible to rate the target job in the future in terms of task importance or time spent. This allows the tasks and knowledge, skills and abilities developed for the present job to be re-rated in the light of these changes. Comparison of present and future ratings can allow an assessment of the degree to which these changes are significant. Such a procedure may be useful also for jobs that do not yet exist, such as new facilities to produce new goods or services. Box 6.1 shows one example.

Assessing and identifying competencies

Recent attempts to identify and assess the key skills and attributes needed by managers and other employees so as to make more effective selection and placement decisions have increasingly focused on the concept of occupational *competencies*. This is characteristic of both US and British approaches, though there are some significant differences as well as similarities between the two perspectives. Job competency in the US tradition has been defined as 'an underlying characteristic of a person which results in effective and/or superior performance in a job' (Boyatzis, 1982), and such competencies are derived through person-oriented job analysis such as 'behavioural event interviews'. The aim has been to identify those characteristics that distinguish superior managerial performance. These are regarded as generic, though receiving different emphases depending on managerial level or sector.

The research underlying this application (Boyatzis, 1982) distinguished between 'threshold' competencies (minimal requirements to do the job at all) and 'differentiators' (those bringing about superior performance). In addition to behavioural event interviews, projective tests of motivation such as the picture story exercise and learning styles inventories were also used. This 'motivational' emphasis seems to be a product of the long-standing interest of David McClelland, the head of McBer

Box 6.1

One UK-based accountancy firm wishing to move towards a more entrepreneurial, market-oriented 'managed business' attempted to identify the skills and qualities required by partners in the *future* as well as in the present.

In the 1980s and 1990s, a large number of mergers took place between firms in the accountancy profession. At the same time, 'middle ground' firms such as Finserv, a medium-sized UK-based accountancy firm, began to feel squeezed between large firms, which were particularly attractive to major companies, and small firms operating in local market niches.

Finserv had grown without much formalized strategic planning; increasingly, however, clients were expecting a full range of services from financial advisers and a detailed knowledge of their particular business. Finserv's chief executive decided that the firm had to become a more 'managed business'. This meant greater emphasis on targets, fee generation, profitability, marketing, accountability and internal controls; it also meant the sacking of non-performing partners and the closure of non-performing regional offices. It was felt that a more entrepreneurial culture was necessary, emphasizing performance-related pay, the importance of success, the identification of selling opportunities, the importance of presentations, networking and liaising with prospective clients and skills in selling on from one service to another. This led to heavy investment in the assessment and development of people, using a competence-based approach.

A major component of the drive to turn Finserv into a more managed business and to develop a more entrepreneurial culture was to use development centres, here termed Assessment for Development Workshops. These used, as criteria, competences identified as necessary for partners to exhibit in the future as well as in the present. Personal feedback and a personal improvement plan against this forward-looking competence profile was offered to all the partners participating in the workshops. The competence approach to cultural change was chosen to encourage identification with the change at a personal level and to promote thought and discussion about the future through the articulation of what the future requirements for success were.

(Shackleton, 1992)

consultancy which carried out the work on behalf of the American Management Association in the late 1970s. He has been particularly interested in motivation and the notion of a basic 'drive for competence', mastery or effectiveness, held to characterize all human beings, and how 'achievement motivation' varies in different cultures and can be developed.

In the British context, such behavioural competencies are often now referred to as 'competencies' rather than competencies and this is the term we shall use here to refer to those aspects of a *person* which can be described as 'behavioural repertoires' which some people can carry out more effectively than others. In this sense, they are to be regarded as 'inputs' into a job and identified through person-oriented job analysis techniques. The 'label' is regarded as a *post-hoc* summary, useful for reducing a myriad of behaviours and a short-hand description, derived either through statistical clustering (e.g. factor analysis) or through more traditional subjective groupings. Such behavioural competencies are regarded as underlying effective performance in a wide range of tasks, sectors and fields. A range of benefits has been claimed from applying such an approach in a wide range of organizations in a wide range of HRM areas (Sparrow, 1994). Such contexts include recruitment and selection, career development, performance management and the management of change. Empirical evidence for these claimed benefits is however less evident.

The UK approach to occupational and managerial competencies as embodied in the work of the National Council for Vocational Qualifications and the Management Charter Initiative is somewhat different. It is more geared to job performance in specific functions and to developing national standards of performance, expressed in terms of outputs rather than inputs. Occupational competence is here defined as the ability to perform the activities within an occupation to the standards expected in employment. These standards are described in terms of elements of competence (which identify a required function), performance criteria (which identify acceptable performance in the function) and range statements (which indicate the contexts in which the standards are to be met). The job analysis technique used – functional analysis – contrasts with the US approach in being task-oriented rather than person-oriented. It identifies the necessary roles, tasks and duties of the *occupation* rather that the skills exhibited by successful role *incumbents*. There is, however, a parallel 'personal competence' model based on person-oriented critical incident and repertory grid techniques which resemble Boyatzis (1982) very closely. The overall British emphasis is much more on minimal standards of performance as exhibited by experienced managers, rather than the characteristics associated with effective or superior managers as in Boyatzis (1982). It is much more linked to job performance in specific functions and is much more geared to certification and accreditation than the US approaches. In this respect it appears to have been influenced by German approaches to apprenticeship and vocational training. The British approach seems much more closely tied than the US approaches to specific qualifications, to accreditation and certification and is closely associated with the accreditation of prior learning (APL).

This particular British approach to vocational education emerged in the 1980s partly as a response to employers' increasing dissatisfaction with the outputs from traditional knowledge-based courses in the light of the increased skill demands of new technology and work practices. The Manpower Services Commission publication *The New Training Initiative: An Agenda for Action* (MSC, 1981) set out a strategy for enhancing the standards of vocational education to develop a more highly skilled and flexible approach, stating that 'at the heart of the initiative lies qualifications of a new kind'. Later publications spelt out a new, more coherent structure of vocational qualifications. For example, a *Review of Vocational Qualifications in England and Wales* (MSC/NEDC, 1986) stated that existing qualifications lacked consistency, clarity and coherence and that a new qualification was necessary, a 'statement of competence, clearly relevant to work and intended to facilitate entry into and progression in employment, further education and training'. A 1986 White Paper led to the formation of the National Council for Vocational Qualifications (NCVQ) and a programme to develop competence-based national students in all vocational areas through 'Lead Bodies' representing a specific functional sector and 'Awarding Bodies' to award NVQs. Stimulated by several reports criticizing the poor UK record in management education and development compared to its leading competitors (e.g. Constable and McCormick, 1987; Handy *et al.*, 1987), the Management Charter Initiative (MCI) was inaugurated in 1988 to act as the lead body for management standards. It developed national standards for three levels of management, supervisory (MIS), Junior (M1) and middle (M2) managers, basing its definition of competence on the NVCQ definition of competence as 'the ability to perform a range of work-related activities and skills, displaying the knowledge and understanding which underpins such a performance to the standards expected in employment'. However, by 1990 while 43 per cent of organizations adopting a competence approach had decided to go down this route, 91 per cent felt negatively about its use for recruitment, 85 per cent for promotion, and 70 per cent for training and development. Many felt the model to be bureaucratic, cumbersome and impractical (Personnel Management, 1990).

Partly in response to criticisms about the devaluation of the role of knowledge and understanding and partly in response to the disappointing take-up rate of its 'products' targeted at supervisory, junior managerial and middle manager levels, MCI appear to have changed tack somewhat in their latest attempts to identify the standards of competence needed by so-called 'strategic' or 'senior' managers (M3), intended to complement the models already in use and to reflect standards of best practice. In addition to developing a set of generic competence-based standards reflecting the role expectations of senior managers using standard functional analysis methodology, it has also attempted to develop 'knowledge and understanding specifications' (KUSPS) and a 'personal competence' model, similar to what we have already termed 'behavioural competency' models. This inclusion of knowledge and understanding and of personal competencies seems a response to earlier criticisms of functional analysis that maintained it neglected personal competencies in being task, rather than person, oriented and that it devalued the importance of knowledge and understanding to 'higher level' work. The operational definition of senior managers was that they would have policy and strategy responsibility, resource responsibility and responsibility for leading strategic change (e.g.

CEO or top team or their direct reports). KUSPS and personal competencies were viewed as 'complementary' to the main competence model, derived primarily from functional analysis. As with the MIS, M1 and M2 frameworks, the first step was to determine the 'key purpose' of senior management, from focus groups and other work. This was held to be to: 'develop and implement strategies and provide leadership to further the organization's mission and achieve the objectives'.

This is depicted as involving four main areas of action:

1 *reading the environment* (identifying and evaluating opportunities and threats in the internal and external environments)
2 *charting the way ahead* (developing and communicating the mission, objectives, goals, values and policies)
3 *planning the action and making the pace* (developing and implementing programme, projects and plans)
4 *evaluation* (reviewing and evaluating objectives and policies).

Focus groups and workshops were held with senior managers from a wide range of UK organizations to identify both the functions undertaken by senior managers and the knowledge and understanding necessary to carry out these functions, primarily using critical incident techniques. These were used to identify outcomes considered to represent successful performance and to identify performance criteria, using outward-looking measures. The personal competencies, or 'underlying abilities which give rise to key behaviours demonstrated by effective senior managers' (Lane and Robinson, 1994: 10) were identified through critical incident and behavioural event analysis, along the lines of Boyatzis (1982). This integrated model is designed to be used to assess and develop senior managers, for senior manager self-development and for organization development (Lane and Robinson, 1994).

Criticisms of competence approaches from the four perspectives

There have been a number of criticisms made of the generic competence models outlined above, whether US or British in origin. One line of criticism is to point out the conceptual ambiguity underlying the term 'competence', since it sometimes seems to refer to behaviours or actions, sometimes to the abilities or characteristics underlying behaviour, and sometimes to the outcomes or results of actions. Interestingly, the distinction between 'performance' and 'competence' was popularized in US behavioural science by Chomsky (1957) in linguistics; the British use of the term seems to make competence synonymous with performance.

Several criticisms have been made by researchers operating from a strategic management perspective. One line of criticism has been to focus on the generic, 'off-the-shelf' nature of existing competency models, arguing that particular sectors, industries and organizational cultures require much more *organization-specific* sets of competencies. This approach has been developed to ensure that employees can identify with the language of the model used and to generate greater staff commitment and ownership. Cadbury-Schweppes, for example, has sought to focus even more closely on competence, as restructuring and delayering have highlighted the importance of managerial skills. It sought to define a 'language of competence' in order to 'find better ways of describing managers' and to help managers gain 'behavioural literacy' (Glaze, 1988: 44). Box 6.2 gives another example, taken from BP.

A second strategic management criticism of many existing competency models is that they are often present or past focused, drawing on what *has* made for successful performance in the past rather than what will make for successful performance in the future. Whether generic or specific, competency models often tend to be historic and retrospective in nature rather than strategic and prospective. A variety of responses have been made to the challenge that, if the essence of the HRM approach is to respond to organizational change and the implications of that change for employee roles and skills, then competence models based on empirical studies of what present managers do and have done will meet the requirements of the past rather than the future. One response has been to identify 'competencies for changing conditions', competencies more suitable for dynamic turbulent environments than those characteristic of more bureaucratic, stable

Box 6.2

BP, in the late 1980s, was undergoing a series of changes, involving increased internationalism, greater emphasis on corporate and national cultures and moves towards enhanced entrepreneurialism, a market orientation and devolved accountability. It sought to identify the key behaviours associated with effective management performance as a way of tapping into the corporate culture, of involving key players and of using the language of organization. The competencies emerging from its analysis (used in such activities as performance appraisal, graduate recruitment, career counselling, profiling and development) were: strategy, drive, relationships, persuasion, leadership, analysis, implementation and such personal factors as integrity and ambition. These were combined with team role performance data (Belbin, 1981) in development initiatives. These competencies emerging through repertory grid and critical techniques were grouped into five clusters:

achievement orientation	personal drive organizational drive, impact, communication
people orientation	awareness of others, team management, persuasiveness
judgement	analytical power, strategic thinking, commercial judgement
situational flexibility	adaptive orientation

The competencies were used alongside personality measures in 'residential assessment boards' and used as a springboard for development initiatives involving feedback, counselling and development options.

In attempting to implement the corporate strategy around an organization-specific, corporate-wide, competency-based model, BP had problems in transferring this Anglo-American model across a variety of national cultures. BP regarded the competencies as generally capable of cross-cultural implementation and as accurately stating the shifts required in management behaviour. The behavioural anchors used to describe specific competencies, however, were sometimes seen as 'culturally provocative'. Different countries were encouraged to offer their own illustrations of how they might change behaviour within the context of the broad competency framework.

127

To manage the enormous diversity created by diversification into minerals, coal, consumer products and information systems, BP in the 1970s created a strong matrix organization focused on business streams and national affiliates. However, this structure appeared to create greater complexity, amplified by privatization and acquisitions. To reduce complexity and change the culture, 'Project 1990' was introduced alongside a corporate-wide competency framework developed by comparing BP with other multinationals. The labels chosen to cluster the sixty seven essential behaviours to enable change to happen were termed OPEN, Open Thinking, Personal Impact, Empowering and Networking. Personal impact for instance refers to Bias for Action, knowing what makes others tick, concern for impact and self-confidence, while Empowerment refers to coaching and developing, building team success and motivating.

(*Source:* Greatorex and Philips, 1990; Sparrow and Bognanno, 1993)

ones. For example, in the USA Schroder (1989) on the basis of complex team simulations attempted to identify 11 'high performance competencies', or observable skills resulting in high levels of performance in changing environments.

This model has been used in the National Westminster Bank (Cockerill, 1989) to link behavioural assessment to unit performance, build teams and cope with the dynamic complex environments characteristic of the financial services sector in the 1990s. Assessments are made on the job and in assessment centres and development programmes installed to enable participants to use strengths, compensate for weaknesses and develop one or two limitations into strengths.

The approach taken by BP and described earlier in Box 6.2 was similar, in that it attempted to identify the competencies which 'enabled change to happen', whatever that change might prove to be (Sparrow and Bognanno, 1993). Similarly, Morgan (1989) on the basis of workshops with a small number of Canadian managers attempted to identify the 'managerial competencies for a turbulent world', that is behaviours that will enable change to happen and enable managers to 'ride the waves of change'.

However, such a list says little about the actual behaviour involved and how managers can do these things *well*, rather than badly. Such a list also seems to lump together skills, attitudes, tasks and functions, and so suffers from the 'ambiguities' referred to earlier in our discussion of the first line of criticism of competence models, their conceptual ambiguity.

The danger of such a list is that the competencies identified are often described in very abstract, generalized terms remote from observable behaviour, making it very difficult for assessors and developers – or managers themselves – to discern how managers are expected to do these things well. Boam and Sparrow (1992) and Sparrow and Bognanno (1993) argue that in many cases organizations will want more specific, focused sets of strategic, future-oriented competencies – not so much 'competencies for change' as 'changing competencies', that is competencies which are specific to particular organizational contexts, situations and environments. The relevance of particular competencies to the organization as a whole or to a particular job or career will shift; so competencies may well exhibit 'life cycles'. Some may be 'emerging', not particularly relevant at present but of growing importance in the future, such as the more commercial skills required by NHS managers since the reforms in the UK National Health Service. Others may be 'mature', becoming of less importance in the future due to strategic shifts, technological change or organization restructuring. Examples might be technical or administrative skills no longer required by managers in privatized industries or 'Next Steps' agencies in the Civil Service. Others may be transitional, relevant to an early stage such as new ventures but perhaps less so as the organization matures. Others may be 'core', of enduring importance and underlying effective performance whatever the strategic direction taken by the organization such as analytical skills. In consequence, competence profiles will have a 'shelf life', though 'the more forward-looking the profile is, the longer its shelf life' (Sparrow and Bognanno, 1993: 56).

A third strategic management criticism of existing competence models is that they give insufficient emphasis to key managerial activities and skills like creativity, impact or sensitivity (termed 'soft' competencies by Jacobs, 1989) which are hard to measure in any circumstances (though they are the kinds of qualities psychometric personality inventories are specifically designed to assess). If Kanter (1989) is right, then such soft competencies as creativity and empathy will become increasingly important to managers in the new organizations.

Analysis of management skills and competencies by Kanungo and Misra (1992) also draws attention to what they term inner resources as components of 'managerial resourcefulness'. Drawing on the analysis of Whitley (1989) of the often emergent, unplanned, unprogrammed, ill-structured and non-routine nature of managerial work, they distinguish between 'skills' and 'competencies' on the basis of several dimensions. These include specific versus generic, task-driven versus person-driven, and transferable versus non-transferable. They argue that managerial resourcefulness has three components: affective, intellectual and action-oriented competence. Affective competence consists of such elements as the self-regulation of emotional reactions under stress, the development of equanimity and of problem solving orientations, the delaying of gratification, and the demonstration of high levels of proactive involvement, enthusiasm and interest in meeting challenges. Intellectual competence refers to applying problem solving strategies and developing self-efficacy. Action-oriented competence refers to the development of goals and plans, the use of feedback, attention to detail, persistence, concern for time, and such people-oriented actions as sensitivity, empathy, active listening, receiving and acting on feedback, adapting non-defensive and supportive postures and using socialized and symbolic influence strategies.

This focus on the 'inner resources' of managers seems to parallel the revival of interest in developing a 'resource-based theory of the firm' discussed in Chapters 1 and 2 (e.g. Grant, 1991). In contrast to conventional theories in strategic management which focus on competitive advantage in the external environment, this perspective places more emphasis on the internal resources and skills of the firm. These resources – including skills, leadership, capital, brand reputation and patents – underlie the capabilities of the organization and its potential for sustainable competitive advantage. This approach to corporate strategy is often associated with the analysis, at the organization level, of 'core competencies' (e.g. Hamel and Prahalad, 1994). In this view, competition is seen as shifting towards functionally based competencies, transcending particular products and able to provide customers with unique benefits and provide a gateway to new opportunities. Once a company has defined its core competence, it needs to define the individual skills and technologies making up that competence. In this sense, models which have their roots in strategic management may look to models derived from more psychometrically rooted conceptions of assessment to operationalize their strategic requirements.

However, it should be noted that more 'purist' psychologists operating from a psychometric perspective are not altogether comfortable with the concept of 'competence', as distinct from the other more accepted constructs in the psychometricians' toolkit, mainly due to conceptual confusion about its meaning. Many competence lists include behavioural and non-behavioural constructs, and even trained observers find it difficult to make clear, discriminating judgements about competencies. One problem appears to be the overlap between the various competencies. For example, assessment centre research shows that assessors find it difficult to evaluate candidates on more than a small number of dimensions. If more than five dimensions are used, large correlations appear between the competencies, suggesting that the competencies are not sufficiently discrete to be useful. Many psychometricians see the psychological theory underpinning competencies as rather limited, in contrast to other, more fundamental, constructs of ability or personality. Robertson *et al.* (1996) note that, despite some claims, there is no evidence to support the existence of a single, universally applicable set of discrete and measurable managerial competencies. Relationships between personality factors and job performance have not tended to generate much in the way of generalizable relationships between specific personality characteristics and managerial performance. The authors sought to explore relationships between indicators of managerial success, specific competencies and personality characteristics. Using a concurrent validation design with 437 managers in five organizations, Robertson *et al.* (1996) used the Saville and Holdsworth Occupational Personality Questionnaire (OPQ) and their Inventory of Management Competencies to

explore links between these predictors and overall job performance and promotability. The competency factors underlying
current proficiency and promotability were different; current
proficiency was most closely related to organization, specialization and analysis displayed by conscientious, intelligent and
introverted people as measured by the OPQ. However, promotability was linked to action/motivation, flexibility/sensitivity
and communication, displayed by employees who were extro-
verted, less conscientious and less agreeable. Cognitive ability
was linked with competencies underlying both promotability
and current proficiency, as was low agreeableness. Purist psychometricians remain uncomfortable with competence as a construct,
preferring more traditional concepts of ability and personality.

A social process view of competencies

As we have seen in Chapter 4, a major concern of the social
process model has been domestic and international diversity and
its implications for assessment practice. A further criticism of
existing competence models is that they are rather parochial and
insular, not international or global. They have developed to describe successful managerial performance in domestic, not global
contexts. However, with the increasing globalization of both
product and labour markets, there is a need to take the ability to
operate cross-culturally into account in any comprehensive model
of managerial competence. We have already seen how BP had to
modify its generic competence model to take account of cultural
differences in Box 6.2. We now need to explore what competencies
are required for international effectiveness. The analysis by
Kanungo and Misra (1982) of 'managerial resourcefulness' finds
an echo in many of the studies of the qualities required for international effectiveness and 'inter-cultural competence'. For example, Rhinesmith (1993) points to the importance of managing
competitiveness, complexity, adaptability, teams, uncertainty and
learning. He also points to the importance of six 'global mindsets':
breadth, balance, process, diversity, change and openness.

A US review of the qualities and skills required for success in
international assignments also points to the importance of not just

job and technical skills but of 'relational dimensions' and 'motivational states' (Ronen, 1989). These are clearly 'inner resources' – tolerance of ambiguity, flexibility, low ethnocentrism, empathy, non-judgementalism, interpersonal skills, interest in other cultures, willingness to acquire new behaviours and attitudes. A Danish review of 'inter-cultural competence' also echoes Kanungo and Misra (1992) in distinguishing affective, cognitive and communicative dimensions (Gersten, 1990). 'Affective competence' refers to similar factors to those identified by Ronen (1990).

A particularly interesting model of the process which may underlie the development of such 'inter-cultural competence' is provided by Ratiu (1983). In order to understand another culture and interact successfully in it, managers must first understand their own culture and its impact on their personal values, attitudes and behavioural styles. Effective international managers tend to be provisional, subjective and relative in their judgements, and are more oriented to finding out *what* is happening rather than *why* it is happening. Less effective international managers, on the other hand, are more judgemental and 'objective' in their approach, using stereotypes unself-consciously and conclusively and attempting to reach rapid conclusions as to 'why' things are happening as they are. They are also less likely to be able to recall and discuss the stress of 'culture shock' and more likely to seek certainty, completeness and rationality. This approach stresses the importance of both 'affective' dimensions of inter-cultural competence and of the cognitive dimensions. This is often termed 'cognitive complexity' or the ability of managers to perceive and categorize the world in general and other people in particular in broad and complex, rather than narrow and simple, ways.

Since managerial work is increasingly likely to require much greater involvement in cross-functional, inter-departmental teams and in strategic alliances with customers, suppliers and other organizations with different 'cultures' and with different ways of seeing things, such an analysis is likely to be applicable to other than transnational situations. Increasingly, managers will be required to display not just task competencies but more general competencies of the kind we have termed 'soft competencies' and 'inner resources'. At present such competencies are often described in terms derived from models of personality traits and assessed through personality inventories. One of the challenges for competency models in the future is to make such 'soft competencies' more behavioural and identifiable in other ways.

A more radical line of criticism of the managerial competence approach from a social process perspective is to argue that individuals are constituted through relations with others, in contrast to traditional competence approaches which posit an additive, static model. These 'assembly models' of building competence links assume that such components can be separated, isolated, described and enumerated. However, alternative approaches to competence see it as constructed in social relationships and social contexts. For example, Pye (1988) argues that a competence is a social construct based on observers attributing competence; it is not something to be 'possessed', rather it is something 'given' by other people in their evaluation of the actions of others in a particular situation at a particular time. What constitutes competence depends on the context and the dynamic changing nature of social interaction, so that any definition of effectiveness must also be relational, dependent on time, context and audience. Any absolute conception of competence or effectiveness must be rejected as 'Both competence and effectiveness are active terms: they are known through action and performance' (Pye, 1988: 64).

To some extent this dynamic processual approach to competence echoes the views of Burgoyne. While recognizing that 'competency approaches have a valuable part to play' (Burgoyne, 1989: 56), he points out eight underlying issues that competence approaches need to address:

- their divisibility and reintegration
- their measurability
- their generalizability
- their ethical and moral content
- their permanence
- their relationship to different styles and strategies of managing
- their relationship to the whole person
- their relationship to collective or organizational competence.

The first seven represent a critique of the 'mechanistic application of a split up list of competencies that assumes a high degree of generalizability over people, situations, organizations, industries and time' (Burgoyne, 1989: 57). Burgoyne himself puts forward a case for a 'management portfolio' approach, based on the creative professions. This kind of approach has become, however, a standard feature of competence-based assessment, especially of APL programmes (accreditation of prior learning). In many cases evidence is accompanied by some kind of 'story board' or personal commentary.

We may term the approach adopted by Pye (1988) and Burgoyne (1989) a 'social process' view of competence. It rejects in particular the view that management is the sequential deployment of discrete competencies in favour of a more holistic approach, one more cognizant of the creative, self-defining nature of the management task. Both also draw attention to the moral, ethical, political and ideological aspects of management, not merely the technical aspects, and to the social, relational, negotiable aspects of the management role. One of the points made by Burgoyne (1989: 60) is that 'high levels of individual member competence do not guarantee group or organization level competence and effectiveness'.

Another trend in these criticisms of competence models is to argue that the dynamic nature of the environment gives existing knowledge and skills a short shelf-life. More emphasis therefore needs to be put on what Burgoyne (1989) calls 'over-arching' or 'meta-competencies', such as learning, adapting, anticipating and creating change. For Brown (1993: 32) these are 'the higher-order abilities which have to do with being able to learn, adapt, anticipate and create, rather than with being able to demonstrate that one has the ability to do'. This discussion echoes the distinction made by Argyris and Schön (1978) between 'single loop' and 'double loop' learning. It suggests that existing competence models are aligned with single loop rather than double loop learning, and that in their focus on 'outcomes' they have neglected 'process' (e.g. Holmes and Joyce, 1993). This emphasis on 'outcomes', as expressed in terms of 'objective standards' carries with it a normative, unitary view of organizations as 'essentially goal directed systems, the parts of which constitute a harmonious whole' (Holmes and Joyce, 1993: 42), a view at odds with empirical research on the essentially political nature of management and organizational processes.

More interactional models of management such as Mangham (1987) reject the idea that competence models can adequately describe a manager's job. He stresses in particular the political and rhetorical skills of managers in the context of the holistic, processual nature of managing as a performing art with no given 'text' but with the possibility of 'personal interpretation'. Burgoyne (1993) also draws attention to the rhetorical and political factors involved in the 'competence movement', mapping some of the major stakeholders as they engage in debates around macro versus micro levels, theoretical versus practical approaches and technical versus political issues. For Burgoyne, the major stakeholders are psychologists (micro, technical), functional analysts, HR managers and directors, educationalists and politicians. Each group relates to the competence models in different ways and uses competence language (or rejects it) to promote certain agendas and interests.

Instead of a 'single stairway', Burgoyne (1993) suggests that 'multiple ladders' of management development are more appropriate: 'learning progresses on different ladders and to different degrees – there is more than one direction to the learning journey, and people, in their development, cover a territory by going different distances in different directions rather than all progressing to a greater or lesser degree down the same broad highway' (pp. 11–12). He concludes by stating that 'competence is a complex and valuable notion, in the sense of creating and executing a valuable performance, but is in danger of being damaged or lost through oversimplification' (p. 13). This sensitivity to the political dimensions of competence are taken further by Townley (1994), who uses a perspective derived from Michel Foucault, and exemplifies a 'radical critical' discourse model of competencies.

A radical critical, discourse view of competencies

The identification of management competencies and the technology for assessing those competencies is seen from this perspective as showing how managers are constituted as managers through a discourse consisting of science-based conceptual frameworks (units of competence identified and distinguished through an elaborate research process involving the opinions of the managers themselves, then formulated in discrete 'real' and relevant elements of human action). These are then allied to a psychologically and psychometrically based technology for the identification, assessment and crucially measurement of individuals against the selected competencies.

The 'knowing' and measurement of individuals in terms of frameworks of managerial competencies is here viewed as an example of the exercise of organizational power – specifically the power of organizational changes and their impact on, and requirements of, individuals, as candidates or employees, and their requirements for individual action and behaviour (Iles and Salaman, 1994).

Townley, for example, argues that recent changes in selection processes and criteria are associated with the focus within HRM on an increased emphasis on 'flexibility', or the requirement for greater exercise of discretion. The changes which have been associated with the introduction of selection and HRM generally have been primarily associated with moves towards 'Japanization' or 'flexibility' and moves away from 'bureaucratized' procedures (Townley, 1989: 106). Townley seeks to make connections between structural (HRM) changes and developments within assessment and selection processes. She argues that developments in selection methods reflect and channel organizational priorities or processes of organizational change. Her analysis therefore focuses on the rationality of these developments, albeit a rationality that is defined in terms of new organizational forms and dimensions of control. However, we can view these processes also as ways in which processes of organizational change and developments in selection criteria and systems cohere and support each other as a set of related and mutually supportive ideas, a discourse which impacts on employees and candidates.

A further and closely related feature of such discourses is that they attend to, define and constitute, the self, the subject (in this case the manager) as composed of measurable quantities of identified competencies. It is precisely by *constituting* rather than opposing the subjectivity of individuals that the power of the organizations is exercised. This discourse which defines managers and managerial competencies creates and shapes individuals as subjects; in this case it constitutes them in terms of the constituent competencies of the 'new' managers as 'required' by the prevalent forms and directions of organizational change discussed in the first part of this book (in Chapter 2 in particular). Furthermore, as Iles and Salaman (1994) point out, the discourse of HRM also constructs a necessary and closed loop of causation: a conception of the environment which requires that organizations develop certain forms of business strategy which in turn needs the support of certain organizational structures, cultures and personnel systems. These in turn require the new competence-based managers. Thus we witness how power works, not against, or in opposition to, the subject (individual versus the state, private versus public, the organization against the employee, etc.) but through the construction, measurement, analysis and treatment of subjectivity.

As Iles and Salaman (1994) argue, the frameworks and associated assessment procedures discussed earlier can be seen to offer a striking instance of the expert constitution of the self. Competencies themselves are presented as real and deep underlying features of humans, *qua* managers. Further organizational progress (the 'career') is based upon evidence that an individual is able to offer that he or she has such competencies. Frequently, disappointed and rejected candidates from the assessment process will be offered counselling or training in order to support them through the trauma of discovery not simply that they have failed a test, but that they lack certain deep qualities. The focus of the discourse therefore is the subjectivity of the individual, defined in terms of qualities and competencies. Individuals are assessed against these, and offered support to develop, or compensation and counselling for lacking, these qualities. Efforts to define and measure managerial competencies represent not only an example of a discourse within an organizational context, but also illuminate aspects and implications overlooked by more traditional discussions of the topic, such as those offered by the psychometric, strategic management and social process models.

The majority of studies focusing on the governmentality of

organizations have chosen to address the nature and impact of 'enterprise' as a significant theme (see Rose, 1990). Such a focus is understandable and valuable, given the undeniable importance of this notion and the discourse surrounding it in contemporary organizational life. However, the focus here is slightly different. While the notion of enterprise undoubtedly serves as a major element, other elements deserve attention. HRM discourses also introduce elements focusing particularly on such key ideas as the importance of 'integration', of achieving a strong culture, of quality, flexibility, and so on, all of which relate to conceptions of the key competencies and responsibilities of management.

CONCLUSIONS

In this book we have examined the management of staff selection and assessment from four different paradigms: strategic management, psychometric, social process and discourse perspectives. All differ, as we have seen, in their understanding of the purpose of assessment in their disciplinary base, in their preferred research methodologies, in their continental origin, in the roles allotted to assessor and assessee, and in the role allotted to assessment instruments. Figure 1 provides a summary of these differences. We then explored one issue of current concern, the assessment of managerial competence, to illustrate how this area was defined and approached differently by the four perspectives.

This book chose to focus first, not on the psychometric perspective within which most selection research has been conducted, but on the strategic management perspective, since most of the current debate on assessment has been driven by the view that rapid environmental change associated with globalization has led to the restructuring of organizations, the redefinition of cultures, and the need to assess the kinds of skills, qualities and other attributes – 'competencies', to use that language – needed by individuals to enable organizations to succeed. Competency frameworks, as we have seen, promise to individualize organizational change and link individual behaviour to strategic

Figure 1 Four perspectives on assessment

	Strategic management	Psychometric	Social process	Critical
Purpose of assessment	Strategic implementation and organizational change	Prediction of job performance. Development of theory	Ongoing relationship Negotiation/renegotiation of contracts	Regulation Government Construction/reconstruction of subjectivity
Disciplinary base	Strategic management	Differential Psychology	Social psychology Interactionist Sociology	Critical theory Sociology
Continental origin	USA	Europe	Europe	
Research methodology	Case study Quantitative survey	Empirical Validation Study Psychometric Test Inventory Scale	Field experiment Interview Observation	Discourse analysis Observation Interview
Role of assessor	Strategic facilitator	Objective measurer	Partner/mentor/co-learner	Regulator Judge/confessor
Role of assessee	Strategic implementer	Passive object	Active agent Mutual participant in contracting	Object of power/knowledge Self regulatory agent
Role of instrument	Strategic change tool Neutral measuring instrument Part of relationship Facilities dialogue	Technology of regulation		

imperatives – so generating a common language linking individual needs with strategic expectations.

The new demands placed on the management of assessment in flatter, delayered, entrepreneurially oriented organizations requiring self-regulating, multi-skilled teams working with empowering managers in a culture of continuous learning and development has challenged those working in a psychometric perspective, with their continuing self-referential commitment to positivist, empiricist research focused on the prediction of performance in stable jobs identified through job analysis and on the measurement of individual differences, conceived of primarily in terms of abstract abilities and personality traits. Purist psychometricians have been reluctant to follow the strategic management 'turn to competence' (du Gay *et al.*, 1996), viewing the competence construct as under-theorized in relation to the long-- established areas of personality and ability measurement and pointing to assessment centre research which appears to show that, whatever their merits as a practical predictor of occupational success (perhaps due to halo, crown prince and self-fulfilling prophecy effects as much as competencies) the conceptual basis for what is actually being measured in a centre remains uncertain (e.g. Robertson *et al.*, 1996). In turn, those psychometricians who have retreated fortress-like into defending their territory like one of the 'besieged' organizations analysed by Miles and Snow (1984) – through developing elegant mathematical models of meta-analysis and utility analysis – have been accused by more 'prospector like' social process theorists like Herriot and Anderson (1997) of becoming outmoded, maladaptive and irrelevant to the concerns of top management and corporate strategy.

The social process theorists argue that the importance of subjectivity and negotiation in assessments, the continuing reliance on the psychometrically derided interview as a focus for two-way interaction, dialogue and mutual negotiation, the empirical research demonstrating the importance of subjective attitudes towards assessment instruments and processes, the effects of assessment processes on self-concepts, attitudes and behaviour and the importance of diversity in assessment in the context of continual contracting and recontracting, all call for a radical change to the psychometric model to incorporate a focus on development rather than selection, on teams and organizations rather than individuals, on self-perceptions rather than on objective assessment, on continual assessment rather than organizational entry, and on a broader range of criteria than supervisors' judgements or promotional success, as well as a broader range of methodologies.

However, their critique is essentially one of adapting and modifying the so-called 'predictivist' model, broadening and extending it so that it is more able than the traditional, closed psychometric paradigm to respond to the new strategic management agenda – an agenda which calls for attention to teams and projects rather than individuals and which has eaten away at the cornerstone of the predictivist paradigm – the job – through the rise of 'joblessness', through short-term project work, 'flexible', contracts, and performance-related and skills-based rather than role-related and job-related pay.

A more fundamental critique of the strategic management and psychometric paradigms is provided by the critical discourse perspective discussed in Chapters 5 and 6, with its focus on power/knowledge shifts, organizational governmentality and the ways in which assessment practices combine with other HRM practices not only to divide, compartmentalize and define the work force as an object of management intervention and knowledge, but also to reconstruct the subjectivity of managers and employees as autonomous, quality-conscious, self-regulating, self-developing and enterprising subjects. They do this not only through the provision of competency frameworks and the assessment of employees against them, but also through extensive feedback, counselling and mentoring processes. As assessment centres in particular are often regarded as accurate, fair and valid, as researchers in the social process traditions have often noted (e.g. Iles and Robertson, 1997), then participants will frequently accept their feedback as accurate and meaningfully construe themselves in terms of it, accept its diagnosis of strengths and weaknesses, use its language, and even act on its recommendations. They may even do this despite seeing assessment centre performance as 'game playing' (e.g. Carter, 1996); even if managers are not aware of the competency frameworks in use in their organization, do not accept them, refuse to buy into or own them, resist them or subvert them for their own purposes and agendas, such frameworks and assessment technologies may still have affect in enabling a particular discourse of organizational change to gain legitimacy and guide both individual and organizational actions.

Du Gay *et al.* (1996) extend this analysis by exploring how current programmes of organization change typically involve radical attempts to reconstitute the nature and conduct of management through the identification of managerial competencies. Organic and flexible organizations, it is argued, need particular capacities and predispositions, especially 'entrepreneurial' capacities. Competence approaches are seen to mediate between structure, and individuals, and define the relationship between the two. Assessment centres and other assessment technologies then operationalize this reconstitution of the manager. One might note also that non-managerial employees in, for example, self-managed teams are also now required to exercise enterprise, self-management and self-regulation, and are subject to more extensive assessment. Economic and organizational priorities are seen as articulated in terms of requisite personal characteristics in the face of environmental change and consequent requirements for 'culture change'. In this climate, managers need to be proactive, self-regulating, and responsible in an organizational environment of quasi-market structures and contractual relationships. Managers in turn are charged with reconstructing the self-image and behaviour of employees in an 'enterprising' direction; their conduct, and that of managers, is shaped and normalized in part through the development of competency frameworks. Competence in this analysis is a technology to instrumentalize and operationalize particular rationalities of government; assessment technologies are used to delineate and assess current levels of competence and enable individuals to manage their own performance as well as their careers. Current conceptualizations of portfolio career management, employability and the new psychological contract represent the values of self-management and self-actualization as personally seductive as well as organizationally desirable.

As du Gay *et al.* (1996: 278) point out, 'contemporary forms of organizational government are premised upon the mobilization of the subjectivity of managers'. Assessment mechanisms constitute an important component in this process, as we have already seen in the utility assessment centre described by Carter (1996).

In this perspective, the discourse of managerial competence provides managers and organizations with a set of assumptions, techniques and data which serve both to make sense of the restructuring of managerial roles and organizations and act as a guide to help managers in such a project. The identification and assessment of competencies through the kinds of assessment processes described in this book is seen to actively contribute to this process, helping both to legitimize it and rationalize it through the appropriation of the 'scientific' language and technology developed in the psychometric traditions.

REFERENCES

Alban-Metcalfe, B. and Nicholson, N. (1984) *The Career Development of British Managers*. London: British Institute of Management Foundation.

Altink, W. M. M., Roe, R. A. and Greuter, A. M. (1991) Recruitment and selection in the Netherlands, *European Review of Applied Psychology*, 41(1), 35–45.

Atkinson, J. (1984) Manpower strategies for flexible organizations, *Personnel Management*, August 28–31.

Argyris, C. and Schön, D. A. (1978) *Organizational Learning: A Theory of Action Perspective*. Reading, Mass: Addison-Wesley.

Armstrong, M. (1993) *Managing Reward Systems*. Buckingham: Open University Press.

Auluck, R. K. and Iles, P. A. (1994) Learning to work with difference. Paper presented to Association for Management Education and Development, Research and Development Conference, Sundridge Park, August.

Baird, L. and Meshoulam, I. (1988) Managing two fits of strategic human resource management, *Academy of Management Review*, 13(1), 116–28.

Beard, D. and Lee, G. (1990) Improved connections at BT's development centre, *Personnel Management*, April, 61–3.

Beaumont, P. B. (1993) *Human Resource Management*. London: Sage.

Belbin, R. (1981) *Management Teams: Why They Succeed Or Fail*. London: Heinemann.

Bevan, S. and Fryatt, J. (1988) *Employee Selection in the United Kingdom*. Brighton: Institute of Manpower Studies.

146

References

Boam, R. and Sparrow, P. R. (eds) (1992) *Designing and Achieving Competency: A Competency-based Approach to Managing People and Organizations*. London: McGraw-Hill.

Boudreau, J. W. (1989) Selection utility analysis: a review and agenda for future research, in M. Smith and I. T. Robertson (eds) *Advances in Selection and Assessment*. Chichester: John Wiley.

Boyatzis, R. E. (1982) *The Competent Manager: A Model for Effective Performance*. New York: John Wiley.

Braich, R. and Iles, P. A. (1994) Managing Diversity. Paper presented to British Psychological Society Occupational Psychology Conference, Brighton, January.

Bridges, W. (1994) *Jobshift: How to Prosper in a Workplace Without Jobs*. Reading, MA: Addison-Wesley.

Brown, R. B. (1993) Meta-competence: a recipe for reframing the competence debate, *Personnel Review*, 22(6), 25–36.

Brown, C. and Gay, P. (1985) *Racial Discrimination 17 Years After the Act*. London: Policy Studies Institute.

Burgoyne, J. (1989) Creating the managerial portfolio: building on competency approaches to management development, *Management Education and Development*, 20, 56–61.

Burgoyne, J. G. (1993) The competence movement: issues, stakeholders and prospects, *Personnel Review*, 22(6), 6–13.

Carter, C. (1996) Rethinking the assessment centre: a technology of power. Paper presented to the British Academy of Management Conference, Birmingham, September.

Chomsky, N. (1957) *Syntactic Structures*. The Hague: Mouton.

Clark, T. (1993) Selection methods used by executive search consultancies in four European countries: a survey and critique, *International Journal of Selection and Assessment*, 1(1), January, 41–9.

Cockerill, A. T. (1989) The kind of competence for rapid change, *Personnel Management*, 21(9), 52–6.

Cockerill, T., Hunt, J. and Schroder, H. (1995) Managerial competencies: fact or fiction? *Business Strategy Review*, 6(3) 1–12.

Commission for Racial Equality (CRE) (1990) *Lines of Progress: An Enquiry into Selection Tests and Equal Opportunities in London Underground*. London: CRE.

Constable, J. and McCormick, R. (1987) *The Making of British Managers*. London: British Institute of Management and Confederation of British Industry.

Davidson, M. J. and Cooper, C. L. (eds) (1984) *Working Women: An International Survey*. Chichester: Wiley.

147

Davidson, M. J. and Cooper, C. L. (1992) *Shattering the Glass Ceiling: The Woman Manager*. London: Paul Chapman.

Deaux, K. and Emswiller, T. (1974) Explanations of successful performance on sex-linked tasks: what is skill for the male is luck for the female, *Journal of Personality and Social Psychology*, 24, 30–85.

de Witte, K., van Laere, B. and Vervaecke, P. (1992) *Assessment Techniques: Towards a New Perspective?* Paper presented to the workshop on Psychological Aspects of Employment, Sofia, Bulgaria, September.

de Wolff, C. J. and Van den Bosch, G. (1984) Personnel selection, in P. J. P. Drenth, H. Thierry, P. J. Williems and C. J. de Wolff (eds) *Handbook of Work and Organisational Psychology*, Vol. 1. Chichester: John Wiley.

di Milia, L., Smith, P. A. and Brown, D. F. (1994) Management selection in Australia: a comparison with British and French findings, *International Journal of Selection and Assessment*, 2(2), 80–90.

du Gay, P., Salaman, G. and Rees, B. (1996) The conduct of management and the management of conduct: contemporary managerial discourse and the constitution of the 'competent' manager, *Journal of Management Studies*, 33(3), 263–82.

Dulewicz, V. (1989) Assessment centres as the route to competence, *Personnel Management*, 21(11), 56–9.

Dye, D. A., Reck, M. and McDaniel, J. (1993) The validity of job knowledge measures, *International Journal of Selection and Assessment*, 1, 3, 153–7.

Eysenck, H. J. (1953) *Uses and Abuses of Psychology*. Harmondsworth: Penguin.

Feltham, R. and Smith, P. (1993) Psychometric test bias: how to avoid it, *International Journal of Selection and Assessment*, 1(2), 117–22.

Fletcher, C. (1991) Candidates' reactions to assessment centres and their outcomes: a longitudinal study, *Journal of Occupational Psychology*, 64, 117–27.

Foucault, M. (1974) *The Archeology of Knowledge*. London: Routledge.

Furnham, A. (1994) The validity of the SHL customer service questionnaire, *International Journal of Selection and Assessment*, 2(3), 157–65.

Gaugler, B. B., Rosenthal, D. B., Thornton, G. C. and Bentson, C. (1987) Meta analysis of assessment centre validity, *Journal of Applied Psychology*, 72(3), 493–511.

Gerstein, M. and Reisman, H. (1983) Strategic selection: matching executives to business conditions, *Sloan Management Review*, 24(2), 33–49.

Gersten, M. (1990) Intercultural competence and expatriates, *International Journal of Human Resource Management*, 1(3), 241–62.

148

References

Glaze, A. (1988) Perfect teams from imperfect people, *Personnel Management*, November, 42–5.

Grant, R. M. (1991) The resource-based theory of competitive advantage: implications for strategy formation, *California Management Review*, 33(3), 114–35.

Greatrex, T. and Phillips, P. (1989) Oiling the wheels of competence, *Personnel Management*, August (21), 36–9.

Hakstian, A. R. and Harlos, K. P. (1993) Assessment of in-basket performance by quality scored methods: development and psychometric evaluation, *International Journal of Selection and Assessment*, 1(3), 135–42.

Hamel, G. and Heene, A. (1994) *Competence-based Competition*. Chichester: John Wiley.

Hamel, G. and Prahalad, C. K. (1994) *Competing for the Future*. Boston: Harvard Business School.

Handy, C., Gow, I., Gordon, C., Randlesome, C. and Moloney, M. (1987) *The Making of Managers*. London: National Economic Development Office.

Hartigan, J. A. and Wigdor, A. K. (eds) (1989) *National Research Council. Fairness in Employment Testing: Validity Generalisation, Minority Issues and the GATB*. Washington, DC: National Academic Press.

Heilman, M. E. and Stopeck, M. H. (1985) Being attractive, advantage or disadvantage?: performance based evaluations and recommended personnel actions as a function of appearance, sex and job type, *Organizational Behavior and Human Performance*, 35, 202–15.

Herriot, P. (1987) The selection interview, in P. B. Warr (ed.) *Psychology at Work*, 3rd edn. Harmondsworth: Penguin.

Herriot, P. (1989a) Selection as a social process, in J. M. Smith and I. T. Robertson (eds) *Advances in Staff Selection*. Chichester: John Wiley.

Herriot, P. (1989b) Interaction with clients in personnel selection, in P. Herriot (ed.) *Assessment and Selection in Organizations: Methods and Practice for Recruitment and Appraisal*. Chichester: John Wiley.

Herriot, P. (1989c) *Recruitment in the 1990s*. London: Institute of Personnel Management.

Herriot, P. (1992) *The Career Management Challenge*. London: Sage.

Herriot, P. (1993) A paradigm bursting at the seams, *Journal of Organisational Behaviour*, 5, 23–6.

Herriot, P. and Anderson, N. (1997) Selecting for change: how will personnel and selection psychology survive?, in N. Anderson and P. Herriot (eds) *International Handbook of Selection and Assessment*. Chichester: John Wiley & Sons.

Hesketh, P. and Robertson, L. (1993) Validating personnel selection: a process model for research practice, *International Journal of Selection and Assessment*, 1(1), 41–9.

Higgs, M. (1988) *Management Development Strategy in the Financial Sector*. London: Macmillan.

Hirsh, W. and Jackson, C. (1990) *Women Into Management: Issues Influencing the Entry of Women Into Managerial Jobs*. Brighton: Institute of Manpower Studies.

Hobson, G. and Lipsett, L. (1993) From service to sales, *International Journal of Selection and Assessment*, 1(3), 170–3.

Hofstede, G. (1980) *Culture's Consequences*. London: Sage.

Hollway, W. (1991) *Work Psychology and Organisational Behaviour*. London: Sage.

Holmes, L. and Joyce, P. (1993) Rescuing the useful concept of managerial competence: from the outcomes back to process, *Personnel Review*, 22(6), 37–52.

Hunter, J. E. and Schmidt, F. L. (1990) *Methods of Meta-analysis*. Newbury Park: Sage.

Iles, P. A. (1991) Using assessment and development centres to facilitate equal opportunity in selection and career development, *Equal Opportunities International*, 8(5), 1–26.

Iles, P. A. (1992) Centres of excellence? Assessment and development centres, managerial competencies and human resources strategies, *British Journal of Management*, 3(2), 79–90.

Iles, P. A. (1997) Sustainable high-potential career development: a resource-based view, *Career Development International*, 2(7), 347–53.

Iles, P. A. and Auluck, R. K. (1991) The experience of black workers, in M. Davidson and J. Earnshaw (eds) *Vulnerable Workers: Psychological and Legal Issues*. Chichester: John Wiley.

Iles, P. A. and Robertson, I. T. (1989) The impact of selection procedures on candidates, in P. Herriot (ed.) *Assessment and Selection in Organisations*. Chichester: John Wiley.

Iles, P. A. and Robertson, I. T. (1997) The impact of personnel selection procedures on candidates, in N. Anderson and P. Herriot (eds) *International Handbook of Selection and Assessment*. Chichester: John Wiley.

Iles, P. A., Robertson, I. T. and Rout, U. (1989) Assessment-based development centres, *Journal of Managerial Psychology*, 4, 11–16.

Iles, P. A. and Salaman, G. (1994) Recruitment, selection and assessment, in J. Storey (ed.) *Human Resource Management: A Critical Text*. London: Routledge.

Jacobs, R. (1989) Getting the measure of managerial competence, *Personnel Management*, October, 32–7.

150

References

Jansen, P. and Stoop, B. (1994) Assessment center graduate selection: decision processes, validity and evaluation by candidates, *International Journal of Selection and Assessment*, 2(4), 193–208.

Janz, T. and Mooney, G. (1993) Interviewer and candidate reactions to patterned behaviour description interviews, *International Journal of Selection and Assessment*, 1(3), 165–9.

Jenson, N. and Mason, D. (1986) Modes of discrimination in the recruitment process: formalisation, fairness and efficiency, *Sociology*, 20, 43–63.

Jenson, N. and Mason, D. (1987) Monitoring equal opportunities policies: principles and practice, in R. Jenkins and J. Solomos (eds) *Racism and Equal Opportunities Policies in the 1980s*. Cambridge: Cambridge University Press.

Jones, A. (1988) A case study in utility analysis, *Guidance and Assessment Review*, 4(3), 3–6.

Jones, R. (1990) Integrating selection in a merged company, *Personnel Management*, September, 38–42.

Kamoche, K. (1994) A critique and a proposed reformulation of Strategic HRM, *Human Resources Management Journal*, 4(4).

Kandola, R. and Cross, R. (1992) From soup to nuts: a radical revision of selection in the employment service. Paper presented to the British Psychological Society Occupational Psychology conference, Merseyside, January.

Kanter, R. M. (1989) The managerial work, *Harvard Business Review*, November–December, 85–92.

Kanungo, R. N. and Misra, S. (1992) Managerial resourcefulness: a reconceptualization of management skills, *Human Relations*, 45(12), 1311–32.

King, N. and Anderson, N. R. (1995) *Innovation and Change in Organizations*. London: Routledge.

Kirton, M. J. (1976) Adaptors and innovators: a description and measure, *Journal of Applied Psychology* (6), 622–9.

Knights, D. and Raffo, C. (1990) Milkround professionalism in personnel recruitment: myth or reality? *Personnel Review*, 19, 28–37.

Kochan, T. A. and Barocci, T. (1985) *Human Resource Management and Industrial Relations*. Boston: Little Brown.

Lane, G. and Robinson, A. (1994) The development of standards of competence for senior management. Paper presented to the Association for Management Education and Development, Henley, September.

Latham, G. P. and Whyte, G. (1994) The futility of utility analysis, *Personnel Psychology*, 47, 31–46.

Latham, G. P., Fay, C. H. and Saari, L. M. (1980) BOS, BES and baloney: raising Kane with Bernardin, *Personnel Psychology*, 33, 815–21.

Luthans, F. and Fox, M. L. (1989) Update on skill based pay, *Personnel*, 66(3), 26–32.

Mabey, C. and Iles, P. A. (1993) The strategic integration of assessment and development practices: succession planning and new manager development, *Human Resource Management Journal*, 3(4), 16–34.

Mabey, C. and Iles, P. A. (1994) *Managing Learning*. London: Sage/Open University Press.

Mabey, C. and Salaman, G. (1996) *Strategic Human Resource Management*. Oxford: Blackwell.

Mangham, I. L. (1987) *Organization Analysis and Development*. Chichester: John Wiley.

Marchese, M. C. and Muchinsky, P. M. (1993) The validity of the employment interview: a meta-analysis, *International Journal of Selection and Assessment*, 1(1), 18–26.

Marshall, J. (1984) *Women Managers*. Chichester: John Wiley.

Miles, R. E. and Snow, C. C. (1984) Designing strategic human resource systems, *Organization Dynamics*, Summer, 36–52.

Miller, P. and Rose, N. (1993) Governing economic life: in M. Gane and T. Johnson (eds) *Foucault's New Domains* pp. 75–105. London: Routledge.

Mintzberg, H. (1973) *The Nature of Managerial Work*. New York: Harper and Row.

Mintzberg, H. (1988) Crafting strategy, *The McKinsey Quarterly*, Summer, 71–89.

Morgan, G. (1989) *Riding the Waves of Change: Developing Managerial Competencies for a Turbulent World*. Oxford: Jossey Bass.

Morrison, A. M. and von Glinow, M. A. (1990) Women and minorities in management, *American Psychologist*, 45(2), 200–8.

MSC (1981) *The New Training Initiative: An Agenda for Action*. Sheffield: MSC.

MSC/NEDC (1986) *Review of Vocational Qualifications in England and Wales*. Sheffield: MSC.

Muchinsky, P. M. (1994) A review of individual assessment methods used for personnel selection in North America, *International Journal of Selection and Assessment*, 2, 118–24.

Murphy, K. R. and Lee, S. L. (1994) Does conscientiousness explain the relationship between integrity and job-performance?, *International Journal of Selection and Assessment*, 2(4), 226–33.

Neter, E. and Ben-Shaker, G. (1989) The predictive validity of graphological inferences: a meta-analytic approach', *Personality and Individual Differences*, 10(7), 737–45.

References

Newell, S. and Shackleton, V. (1992) The use and attitudes to psychometric tests: a comparison of the UK and Germany. Paper presented to the British Psychological Society Occupational conference, Liverpool.

Nicholson, N. (1984) A theory of work-role transitions, *Administrative Science Quarterly*, 29, 172–91.

Paddisan, L. (1990) The targeted approach to recruitment, *Personnel Management*, November, 55–58.

Papalexandris, N. (1991) A comparative study of human resource management in selected Greek and foreign owned subsidiaries in Greece, in C. Brewster and S. Tyson (eds) *International Comparisons of Human Resource Management*. London: Pitman Publishing.

Paton, R. and Hooker, C. (1990) *Developing Managers in Voluntary Organizations: A Handbook*. Sheffield: Open University and Employment Department.

Pearn, M. and Kandola, R. (1992) *Job Analysis: A Manager's Guide*. London: Institute of Personnel Management.

Personnel Management (1990) Management Charter Initiative has had little impact so far, *Personnel Management*, 22(1), 14.

Pollert, A. (1988) The flexible firm, *Warwick Papers in Industrial Relations*, no. 19. Coventry: University of Warwick.

Porter, M. E. C. (1980) *Competitive Strategy*. New York: Free Press.

Powell, G. N. (1993) *Women and Men in Management*, 2nd edn. Newbury Park: Sage.

Purcell, J. (1989) The impact of corporate strategy on human resource management, in J. Storey (ed.) *New Perspectives on Human Resource Management*. London: Routledge.

Pye, A. (1988) Management competence in the public sector, *Public Money and Management*, Winter, 62–7.

Ratiu, I. (1983) Thinking internationally: a comparison of how international executives learn, *International Studies of Management and Organization*, 14(1–12), 139–50.

Rhinesmith, S. (1993) *A Manager's Guide to Globalization*. Arlington, UA: ASTD/Irwin.

Robertson, I. and Gibbons, P. (1996) Understanding management performance. Paper presented to the British Academy of Management Conference, Aston, September.

Robertson, I. R. and Iles, P. A. (1988) Approaches to management selection, in C. L. Cooper and I. Robertson (eds) *International Review of Industrial and Organisation Psychology*. Chichester: John Wiley.

Robertson, I. T. and Kandola, R. S. (1982) Work-sample tests: validity, adverse impact and applicant reaction, *Journal of Occupational Psychology*, 55, 171–83.

Robertson, I. T. and Makin, P. (1986) Management selection in Britain: a survey and critique, *Journal of Occupational Psychology*, 59, 45–57.

Robertson, I. T. and Sadri, G. (1993) Managerial self-efficacy and managerial performance, *British Journal of Management*, 4, 37–45.

Robertson, I. T., Iles, P. A., Gratton, L. and Sharpley, D. (1991) The psychological impact of selection procedures on candidates, *Human Relations*, 44(9), 963–82.

Roger, D. and Mabey, C. (1987) BT's leap forward from assessment centres, *Personnel Management*, July (19), 32–5.

Ronen, S. (1989) Training the international assignee, in I. Goldstein (ed.) *Training and Development*. San Francisco: Jossey Bass.

Rose, M. (1988) *Industrial Behaviour*. Harmondsworth: Penguin.

Rose, N. (1985) *The Psychological Complex*. London: Routledge.

Rose, N. (1990) Governing the soul. Paper presented to the conference on the Values of the Enterprise Culture, University of Lancaster.

Rosener, J. B. (1990) Ways women lead, *Harvard Business Review*, November–December, 119–25.

Rowe, P. M., Williams, M. C. and Day, A. L. (1994) Selection procedures in North America, *International Journal of Selection and Assessment*, 2(2), 74–9.

Ryan, A. M. and Sackett, P. R. (1987) A survey of individual assessment practices by I/O practitioners, *Personnel Psychology*, 40, 455–88.

Salaman, G. and Butler, J. (1990) Why managers won't learn, *Management Education and Development*, 21(3), 183–91.

Salaman, G. and Thompson, K. (1978) Class culture and the persistence of an elite: the case of army officer selection, *The Sociological Review*, 26(2), 283–304.

Salaman, G. (ed.) (1992) *Human Resource Strategies*. London: Sage.

Schein, V. E. (1973) The relationship between sex role stereotypes and requisite management characteristics, *Journal of Applied Psychology*, 57, 95–100.

Schein, V. E. (1978) Relationships between sex-role and requisite management characteristics among female managers, *Journal of Applied Psychology*, 60, 340–4.

Schein, V. E. (1989) Sex role stereotypes and requisite management characteristics past, present and future. Paper presented at the Current Research in Women in Management Conference, Queen's University, Ontario, Canada, September 24–6.

Schmidt, N. and Hill, T. E. (1977) Sex and race composition of assessment centre groups as a determinant of peer and assessor ratings, *Journal of Applied Psychology*, 62, 261–4.

References

Schroder, M. (1989) *Managerial Competence: The Key to Excellence.* Dubuque, Iowa: Kendall and Hunt.

Schuler, R. S. (1989) Strategic human resource management and industrial relations, *Human Relations*, 42(2), 157–84.

Schuler, R. S. and Jackson, S. (1987) Linking competitive strategies with human resource management practices, *Academy of Management Executive*, 1(3), 209–13.

Schuler, H., Frier, D. and Kauffman, M. (1992) Strategic human resources management: linking the people with the strategic needs of the business, *Organizational Dynamics*, 21(1), 18–22.

Shackleton, V. (1992) Using a competency approach in a business change setting, in R. Boam and P. Sparrow (eds) *Focussing on Human Resources: A Competency-based Approach.* London: McGraw-Hill.

Shackleton, V. and Newell, S. (1991) Management selection: a comparison survey of methods used in top British and French companies, *Journal of Occupational Psychology*, 64(1), 23–6.

Shackleton, V. and Newell, S. (1994) European management selection methods: a comparison of five countries, *International Journal of Selection and Assessment*, 2(2), 91–102.

Silverman, D. and Jones, J. (1973) Getting in: the managed accomplishment of 'correct' selection outcomes, in J. Child (ed.) *Man and Organisation.* London: Allen and Unwin.

Silverman, D. and Jones, J. (1976) *Organisational Work.* London: Collier Macmillan.

Smith, E. J. (1990) Developing business men and women in financial services, *CBSI Journal*, 198(344), 4–7.

Smith, M. and Robertson, I. T. (1989) *Advances in Selection and Assessment.* Chichester: Wiley.

Sonnenfeld, J. A. and Pieperl, M. A. (1988) Staffing policy as a strategic response: a typology of career systems, *Academy of Management Review*, 13, 588–600.

Sparrow, P. (1994) Organizational competencies: creating a strategic behavioural framework for selection and assessment, in N. Anderson and P. Herriot (eds) *Assessment and Selection in Organizations: First Update.* Chichester: John Wiley & Sons.

Sparrow, P. R. and Bognanno, M. (1993) Competency requirement forecasting: issues for international selection and assessment, *International Journal of Selection and Assessment*, 1(1), 50–8.

Sparrow, P. and Pettigrew, A. (1988) Strategic human resource management in the UK computer supplier industry, *Journal of Occupational Psychology*, 61(1), 25–42.

Sparrow, P., Grattan, L. and McMullan, J. (1989) *Human Resource Issues in Information Technology*. PA Consulting Group, BT, February.

Thacker, J. W. and Cattaneo, R. J. (1993) *Survey of Personnel Practices in Canadian Organisations: A Summary Report to Respondents*. Working paper series no. W92-04. Windsor, Ontario: University of Windsor.

Tichy, N. M., Fombrun, C. J. and Devanna, M. A. (1982) Strategic human resource management, *Sloan Management Review*, 23(2), 47–61.

Townley, B. (1989) Selection and appraisal: reconstituting 'social relations', in J. Storey (ed.) *New Perspectives on Human Resource Management*. London: Routledge.

Townley, B. (1994) *Reframing Human Resource Management*. London: Sage.

Vernon, P. E. and Parry, J. B. (1949) *Personnel Selection in the British Forces*. London: University of London Press.

Waterman, R., Waterman, J. and Collard, B. A. (1994) Towards a career-resilient workforce, *Harvard Business Review*, July–August, 87–95.

Wernimont, P F. and Campbell, J. P. (1967) Signs, samples and criteria, *Journal of Applied Psychology*, 52, 373–6.

Whitley, R. (1989) On the nature of managerial tasks and skills: their distinguishing characteristics and organization, *Journal of Management Studies*, 26(3), 209–24.

Williams, A. P. O. and Dobson, P. (1995) Personnel selection and corporate strategy, in P. Herriot (ed.) *Assessment and Selection in Organizations*, 2nd Update and Supplement. Chichester: Wiley.

Woolley, R. M. and Hakstian, A. R. (1993) A comparative study of integrity tests: the criterion-related validity of personality-based and overt measures of integrity, *International Journal of Selection and Assessment*, 1(1), 27–40.

Windholf, P. and Wood, S. (1988) *Recruitment and Selection in the Labour Market*. Aldershot: Avebury.

Wood, R. (1994) Work-samples should be used more (and will be), *International Journal of Selection and Assessment*, 1(3), 170–3.

Woodruffe, C. (1990) *Assessment Centres: Identifying and Developing Competence*. London: Institute of Personnel Management.

Wright, P. M., Lichtenfels, P. A. and Pursell, E. D. (1989) The structured interview: additional studies and a meta-analysis, *Journal of Occupational Psychology*, 62, 191–9.

Wright, P. M., McMahan, G. C. and McWilliams, A. (1994) Human resource management and sustained competitive advantage, *International Journal of Human Resource Management*, 5(2), 301–26.

INDEX

157

Index

in the Netherlands, 74, 82
patterned behaviour
    description, 61, 67
and predictive validity, 64, 65
situational, 62–3, 64, 67, 74
and the social process model,
    80
structured, 19, 22, 64, 65, 67, 68,
    108
and the technology of power,
    110
in the UK, 81
unstructured, 65, 67, 68, 85, 108,
    111
in the USA, 85, 99
and women managers, 95
inventories, 69–71
    see also personality inventories
Israel, 64
IT (information technology)
    industry, and strategic
    management, 31–6
Italy, 83, 86

Japanese companies, and
    competence management
    skills, 16–17
job, as a set of specific tasks, 19, 20,
    106, 107, 119
job analysis, 2, 7, 8, 9, 10–11, 13, 142
    and assessment centres, 73
    equal opportunity
        considerations, 87, 90
    examining present behaviour
        and skills, 62
    explicit, 53, 55
    implicit, 53, 54
    and managerial competencies,
        118–20
    and the managerial self-efficacy
        scale, 63
    and matrix forms, 40

and occupational competence,
    123
person-oriented, 119, 122
and the psychometric
    perspective, 18, 20, 22, 76,
    77, 108
and the recruitment of women
    managers, 94
strategic, 119–20
task-oriented, 119
as a technology of power, 110
job description, 87, 119
job design, 7, 8, 30, 60
job evaluation, 20
job flexibility, 53, 54
'job knowledge' tests, 69
job performance, see performance
job redesign, 2, 7
job roles, 2
job rotation, and prospector firms,
    45
job security, and financial services
    organizations, 52
jobless society, 20
jobshift, 20
justice, procedural and
    distributive, 99–100

knowledge
    and power, 2, 28, 29, 109–11,
        114–15
    tests, in Flanders (Belgium), 82

leadership, and managerial
    competencies, 43
legal and regulatory frameworks,
    and HRM practice in
    Germany, 84, 86, 103
life-cycle model
    of competencies, 129
    of strategic assessment, 41–4, 57,
        58, 60

163

Index

older people, evaluating
   assessment methods for
   bias against, 65
OPQ (Saville and Holdsworth's
   Occupational Personality
   Questionnaire), 69–70,
   131–2
organizational change, 9, 11–12,
   31, 140–2
   and competency models, 126–9,
   137, 144
   and job analysis, 119
   and managerial competencies,
   115
   and matrix forms, 40–1
   and the psychometric
   perspective, 107
   by strategic type, 46–7
organizational climate, 8
organizational competence, 135
organizational culture, 2, 11
   and matrix forms, 40–1
organizational design structure
   and assessment, 39–41
organizational development, 8–9,
   9
organizational effectiveness, 3, 8,
   12
   and individual differences in
   performance, 101
organizational leadership, and
   managerial competencies,
   43
Organizational Management
   Reviews, 37
organizational psychologists, and
   national practices, 86
organizational strategy, 1
   and assessment strategies, 41–7,
   96
organizational structure, 1–2, 11, 60
   and assessment, 30, 39–41, 58

and managers' way of working,
   118
outcomes, and processes, 135–6

part-time employees, 53, 105
past-oriented methods, of
   selection and assessment,
   61–2
pay
   equal, 88, 90
   performance-related, 117
peer assessment, 62, 64
performance
   assessing future, 62–3
   prediction of, 13, 64, 106, 111
      and inventories, 69–70, 71
      and tests, 69
   promotion and past
      performance, 11
   and the psychometric
      perspective, 19, 20, 21, 22, 76
   and the social process model, 96
performance appraisal, 7, 12
performance management, 8
performance review, 12
performance-related pay, 117
peripheral workers, 105
person-oriented job analysis, 119,
   122
personality characteristics, and
   managerial competence,
   131–2
personality inventories, 9, 18, 62,
   65, 69, 70–1, 76, 110
   in Flanders (Belgium), 82
   in the USA, 85
   and women managers, 95
personality tests
   in Canada, 85
   in Flanders (Belgium), 82
   in France, 83
   in Greece, 84

Index

turnover
  at clubs and academies, 50
  and baseball-team firms, 48, 50
  reducing, 12

uncertainty avoidance, 85, 86
United Kingdom
  British textile industry, 46
  building society industry, 32–5, 36, 47, 51
  central and local government, 38
  Civil Service, 49, 129
  and European Union equality legislation, 88
  financial services industry, 31, 32–5, 47, 98, 128
  IT industry, 31–6
  National Health Service, 129
  national practices, 81–2
  occupational competencies, 120, 121, 122
  and the psychometric perspective, 17, 104
  public sector, assessment centres, 74–5
  racial discrimination, 88–9
  selection of British army officers, 25–6
  and situational interviews, 63
  vocational education, 123–5
  women managers, 94, 95–6
United States
  assessment methods, 63
  competencies and organizational change, 128
  differential psychology, 12
  equal opportunity considerations, 21, 88, 90, 107
  and job competency, 120–2

national practices, 84–5
  and the psychometric perspective, 17, 18, 23, 105–6
  and situational interviews, 63
  social psychological research studies, 99–100
  women managers, 94
utility theory, 77, 79, 103
  and the social process model, 80

validity, 63–6, 77
  of assessment centres, 64, 73–4, 77
  generalization, 80, 108
  of interviews, 68
  of tests, 69
validity coefficient, 64
validity generalization, 77
vocational education, British approach to, 123–5

Williams, A.P.O., 57–8
women
  managers, 90, 91, 93–6
  possible bias against, 65, 106
    and assessment centres, 73
    and interviews, 67
  recruitment of, 91, 92
work experience, 53
  and job performance, 106–7
work samples, 62, 64, 65, 77, 108
  in Canada, 85
  and equal opportunity considerations, 90
  tests, 72–3, 82
  in the USA, 85
  see also assessment centres
work-based learning, 98

Zimbabwe, 104